THE LAST ALASKAN BARREL

ARCTIC REGION

Courtesy of the University of Texas Libraries, the University of Texas at Austin.

THE LAST ALASKAN BARREL
An Arctic Oil Bonanza that Never Was

GLENN —
THIS IS ABOUT
THE SECOND TOUGHEST
BUSINESS AFTER
FILMS.

[signature]

John M. Miller

Caseman Publishing • Anchorage, Alaska

Printed in the United States of America
First Printing: September 2010

Caseman Publishing
Anchorage, Alaska
www.thelastalaskanbarrel.com

Copyright ©2010 by John M. Miller
ISBN: 978-0-9828780-0-2
Library of Congress Control Number: 2010910494

Cover and interior design and layout by Stephen Tiano, Book Designer
    http://www.tianobookdesign.com
Edited by Arlene Prunkl, Kelowna, B.C., Canada
Indexed by Clive Pyne, Ottawa, Ontario, Canada

Contents

Alaskan Oil System

Prudhoe Bay, the largest petroleum reservoir in North American history, and several smaller oilfields are located on state-owned land between the National Petroleum Reserve—Alaska (NPR–Alaska) to the west and the Arctic National Wildlife Refuge (ANWR) to the east. The 1002 Area is the coastal portion of ANWR endlessly debated for exploratory drilling. The 800-mile Trans-Alaska Pipeline System (TAPS) transports crude oil from the Arctic coast to the ice-free port of Valdez. Through 2009, more than 20 thousand ocean tanker shipments had carried 16 billion barrels from Valdez to mostly domestic refineries thousands of miles away.

Preface

With constant talk about "exorbitant profits" for oil companies and "pain at the pump" for consumers, it seems reasonable to assume that Alaskan oil has proven to be a bonanza. Yet, contrary to popular belief, it has been a financial disappointment for the companies and their shareholders that risked billions of dollars to make it happen. In fact, if oil companies had known at financing what they know today about prices, costs, and taxes, they would never have developed Alaskan oil over the last fifty years.

State leaders anticipated potential riches when they selected land on the Arctic coastal plain in the vicinity of Prudhoe Bay as part of the statehood pact of 1959. The federal government made Alaska the 49th state partly because future oil revenue might reduce the amount of federal subsidy required to manage it as a territory. With confirmation of large reserves near Prudhoe Bay in 1968, oil was destined to become the dominant force in the economics and politics of Alaska for decades.

Early on, many claimed Arctic development posed an environmental dilemma. Some still do. While there have been trade-offs and a few human errors, the "Great Land" remains beautiful and virtually pristine.

The standard of living for Alaskans is higher than ever. The caribou herd has grown by a factor of thirteen. Salmon are spawning, while bear, moose, and caribou wander the state unfettered. Though once feared, no fast-food restaurants or billboards exist along the pipeline route.

Rather than posing an environmental dilemma, Alaskan oil has presented a profit *trilemma* instead. That is, how to fairly share the value of billions of barrels among three major stakeholders: the state of Alaska, the federal government, and the oil companies that take the investment risk.

Despite the state's good fortune, anti-oil company sentiment in Alaska has been increasing in inverse proportion to declining production. Elected leaders and newspaper editorial pages claim the state never got its fair share of the profits as fear of a future without oil grows.

Whenever energy prices spike higher, so does national political debate about drilling in ANWR. There are dreams of finding another giant reservoir or building a natural gas pipeline to the Lower 48. It is implicitly assumed by just about everyone that oil companies cannot wait to garner more huge profits in Alaska. On the contrary, in light of the first fifty years of Arctic experience, it is becoming increasingly likely that the bulk of the remaining petroleum resource will go undeveloped.

Every late September, termination dust, a light layer of snow on mountain peaks, signals a fast-approaching winter in subarctic Alaska. Autumn in the Anchorage Bowl, home to nearly one-half of Alaska's population of 670 thousand (2009 estimate), is short. Leaves change color and fall at time-lapse speed.

In mid-November, 650 miles away, seven thousand residents of eight small Arctic villages and a few oil workers see their last sunlight for more than two months. Although there are no mountains to sprinkle with snow on the Arctic coastal plain, there are clear signs of another kind of termination dust. Oil production in Arctic Alaska is in steep decline.

The Last Alaskan Barrel begins with abridged histories of Alaska and the oil age leading to exploration of the Arctic. This is followed by the dramatic discovery of large oil deposits near Prudhoe Bay. A White House study follows, claiming the nation is swimming in cheap Alaskan crude. "Expert" opinions abound. There is a rush to find more, and a near-decade ordeal to get Arctic oil to consumers.

This book examines how, when crude finally flows, stake-holders breathe a brief sigh of relief. However, the economic ordeal has only just begun. An updated federal study just before start of production has contradicted the earlier White House study. The new study says that Alaskan oil is expensive and a marginal investment just as companies had claimed from the start. Over the next decades, oil prices, development costs, and a variety of taxes further shrink the size of the prize.

Finally, the actual investment return for Alaskan oil is com-pared to other investments. The distribution of profits among the state of Alaska, the federal government, and oil companies is shown. The book concludes with a glimpse at future oil and natural gas potential in Arctic Alaska.

Matthew R. Simmons, in *Twilight in the Desert* (Wiley 2005), writes that the time has come for energy analysts to calculate real-market economics (page 346). *The Last Alaskan Barrel* does just that. It is thoroughly researched by an author who directed technical and economic analyses of Alaskan oil and can clarify the issues. The book includes extensive references gathered from public sources. The material is accessible to readers unfamiliar with petroleum and economics.

Petroleum is coming from more remote, costly, challenging, and government-controlled sources worldwide. For over three decades, an average one-fifth of domestic oil production in the U.S. has come from 9 thousand feet under the tundra of Arctic

Alaska, just more than a thousand miles from the North Pole. Understanding the fifty-year investment life of Alaskan oil finally brings unemotional, objective clarity to the complex world of energy economics.

Acknowledgments

*T*he *Last Alaskan Barrel* is a case study of the risk and uncertainty of America's premier petroleum development. It is dedicated to the thousands of people from hundreds of worldwide companies that made the extraordinary and impossible become matter of fact. Despite extreme conditions, Arctic Alaskan oil has been reliably transported thousands of miles to domestic consumers for more than three decades. Yet this astounding achievement on Earth's version of a moonscape is taken more for granted by the public than even the nation's space program.

Writing a book is also fraught with risk and uncertainty. I owe a debt of gratitude to my wife, Susie, who, after twenty-five years, continued to surprise me with hidden skills and provided a sounding board night and day. My daughter, Katlyn, checked in from afar every day for nearly four years, stayed involved, and reviewed an early draft manuscript for her senior honors program at The American University in Washington, D.C. Many thanks are due Dr. Augusta Gooch and Dr. Deborah Heikes, professors at the University of Alabama-Huntsville, who were the first non-industry reviewers of a draft manuscript. Their enthusiastic, constructive, and pleasantly surprising feedback was an inspiration for me to press on.

Real energy-industry experts, with nearly a century of combined knowledge, are friends and longtime colleagues—Leigh Noda, Rich Pittman, and Ken Rupp. We lived together through the early days of Atlantic Richfield Company and were dedicated to the perfection of Alaska North Slope development from the beginning. Leigh, Rich, and Ken brought decades of experiences from wide-ranging assignments around the world including engineering and project management, planning and financial analysis, and refining and marketing to the manuscript review process.

Their advice added clarity and depth, engineering and financial expertise, laughs and memories, and clear focus. They supplied the blend of encouragement, seasoned analysis, and stress-breaking humor representative of the unique people who pulled off the impossible in Arctic Alaska with little to no public recognition. We share unforgettable memories from decades of work with thousands of proud, unsung people on the hostile, frozen tundra who struggled to make America more energy self-sufficient.

As analysts and engineers, we are trained to ask the right question. In the final analysis, *The Last Alaskan Barrel* asks and answers whether the first fifty years of Alaska North Slope development was really worth the investment risk for the original oil companies and their shareholders. As with most objective analysis, fact and reality are often quite different from popular opinion and perception.

ONE

Profits Trilemma

Alaska is a tale of two very different economic times, before and after Prudhoe Bay oil. Initially, small, diverse groups of indigenous peoples sparsely populated *Alyeska,* an Aleut word meaning "Great Land." Their lives remained virtually constant and untouched by outsiders for thousands of years.

By the late 1700s, neighboring Russia had staked a claim on *Alyeska* to harvest Aleutian Island seals for their fur pelts. When fur profits for the Pacific trade plummeted a few decades later, Russia dealt its North American holding to the United States. *Alyeska* became Alaska. Geographical isolation, an inhospitable climate, and immense size limited access to most of the vast cache for centuries—until Prudhoe Bay oil.

In 1959, Alaska became America's 49th state, coincidentally at the start of the second century of the commercial oil age. By then, the center of gravity of world petroleum was shifting from the Americas toward the Middle East and Russia. Suddenly, there was a slight shift back to the west.

On a bitterly cold day just after Christmas 1967, a drilling rig found natural gas on the Arctic coast near Prudhoe Bay.

After a few more weeks of drilling, the rig penetrated a thick oil layer approximately 9 thousand feet below the frozen tundra, effectively ending the first Alaska. Since then, modern Alaska has depended on oil revenue created by billions of dollars of investments made by oil companies and their shareholders.

Alaska remained financially challenged following its purchase from Russia in 1867 until the start of Prudhoe Bay production in 1977. What resource revenue there was came from occasional boomlets of minerals and salmon spawning cycles. The poems of Robert Service and the short stories of Jack London portray the romantic lore of pioneer Alaska and Canada. In reality, the Klondike gold rush of the late 1890s is insignificant in the economic history of Alaska. The same goes for copper, salmon, timber, and anything else. A professor of history at the University of Alaska Fairbanks put it best: "The balance sheet of Alaskan economic history is simple: one Prudhoe Bay is worth more in *real* [inflation-adjusted] dollars than everything that has been dug out, cut down, caught, or killed in Alaska since the beginning of time."[1]

Similar to Saudi Arabia, petroleum exports have financed an average 85 percent of the state's annual discretionary spending.[2] Thanks to oil production, residents of Alaska avoid paying either a state income or a statewide sales tax. The state constitution requires investment of at least one-fourth of the oil royalties with the Alaska Permanent Fund Corporation, a professionally managed sovereign wealth fund. Since late 2008, the state invests one-half. The principal reached $40 billion during 2007 before falling in early 2009 as low as $26 billion during the worldwide financial meltdown.[3] By mid-2010, the fund had recovered to between $34 and $35 billion. Every Alaskan receives an annual Permanent Fund Dividend (PFD) check just for breathing.

In the final analysis, 75 percent of Alaska's cumulative resource wealth in *nominal* (not inflation-adjusted) dollars has come from oil in the short time since 1977.[4] Moreover, about three-fourths of all resource value has come from the Prudhoe Bay oilfield alone. A display of historical resource value from 1867 through 2007 is remarkable.

Alaska Resource Value (1867–2007)

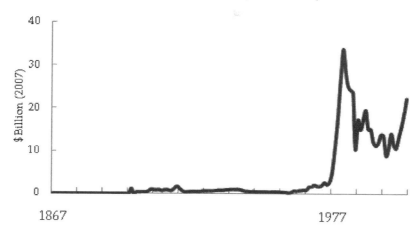

Data Source: Alaska Department of Natural Resources.

Resource value is shown in real dollars as of 2007, denoted as $ (2007). Dollar values not identified as real are nominal dollars, which represent the dollar value at the time. Multi-decade investments and economic analyses start with dollars that are more valuable and end with less valuable ones as inflation erodes the nominal value. Real dollars are inflation-adjusted to a date such as 2007. Real dollars measure future investment power that nominal dollars do not. For example, it took more than seven dollars in 2007 to equal the value of one dollar in 1959, the first year of Alaskan statehood. Put another way, multi-decade investments need to earn more dollars in the future to pay out early investment dollars.

Historians often refer to the Great Land's economic history as one of a series of booms and busts. In reality, there has been only one boom in Alaska—Prudhoe Bay oil.

Russian America

In the late 1500s, Flemish cartographer Gerardus Mercator mapped a possible water passage connecting Asia and Europe, the Northwest Passage. The idea that it could exist had been around since ancient Roman times. Circa Mercator, Venetian cartographer Giacomo Gastaldi depicted a strait separating the continents of Asia and North America at the "end of the world." These conceptual views piqued the interests and catalyzed the actions of explorers from Russia, England, and Spain. Since then, historians have recorded several European "discoveries" of the waterway separating the continents and numerous attempts to sail a Northwest Passage over the top of Canada and Alaska.

In 1728, Vitus Bering, a Dane serving in the Russian Navy, and his crew sailed north through the strait envisioned by Gastaldi until they reached ice. They came within fifty miles of what is now Alaska but missed a sighting due to whiteout conditions of fog and ice mist. Recent research by Russian scholars has confirmed, however, that Semyon Dezhnyov sailed part of the Intercontinental Divide from north to south eighty years before Bering in 1648.

Fifty years after Bering, English Captain James Cook named the strait for his fellow navigator and naval man, even though Cook was aware of the earlier trip by Dezhnyov. Cook wrote, "In justice to the memory of Bering, I must say that he has delineated the coast very well, and fixed the latitude and longitude of the points better than could be expected by the method he had to go by."[5]

In 1790, Spain tossed her hat into the *Alyeska* ring. Cartographer Lt. Salvador Fidalgo sailed into Prince William Sound to investigate advances by Russia and Britain and claimed *Alyeska* for Spain. Fidalgo named Cordova, Port Gravina, and the Bay of Valdez (pronounced *Valdeez* by Alaskans) after the leader of the Spanish marines. However, Spain had overextended its reach and eventually retreated to California, leaving the future of *Alyeska* to the others.[6]

Sir John Franklin, a British explorer and naval officer, discovered a Northwest Passage through the Arctic Ocean connecting the Atlantic and Pacific Oceans and made three unsuccessful attempts to navigate one. On his second expedition (1825–1827),

Franklin approached the Arctic coast from the Mackenzie River in Canada. From the mouth of the Mackenzie, he sent two boats east while he headed west in another.

When ice and fog made sailing impossible, he surveyed another 400 miles of the shoreline on foot before turning back at an inlet he named Prudhoe Bay.[7] His journal referred to a sticky substance he found along the way: "I found this evening that a piece of the petroleum or bitumen which I had picked up at Garry's Island had become much softened by being in my pocket and that it had stuck to the powder horn in the same pocket ... "[8]

By the 1840s, British explorers had mapped most of the Arctic coast but had not navigated a Northwest Passage. The British Admiralty selected Franklin for that crowning achievement. However, on his third try (1845–1847), Franklin and his 128-man crew perished.

For more than a decade, 32 rescue and then search missions looked for evidence of Franklin and his crew's fate while gaining more knowledge of the Arctic along the way. The last mission found logbooks confirming Franklin's death and came across a few skeletons.[9] Franklin's statue stands incognito (the plaque fell off) on the grounds of the Anchorage Public Library gazing north toward Prudhoe Bay.

In November 1977, Soviet Ambassador to the United States Anatoly Dobrynin, and his wife, Irina, made an unofficial trip to Alaska. For a few days, the Dobrynins toured newly commissioned production facilities and the brand new Trans-Alaska Pipeline System (TAPS). After panning for some gold in the western village of Nome, their trip ended at the former Russian America capital of *Novo Arkhangelsk* or New Archangel in southeastern Alaska, now known as Sitka.

Reporters asked Dobrynin for some reflections at the place where Russian America had become a United States possession just over a century earlier. He lamented the 1867 sale for $7.2 million by Tsar Alexander II noting it " ... was known as Seward's

Folly, but Alexander was known as foolish in my own country long before he sold Alaska. Sometimes we feel it's another proof of how stupid tsars were."[10]

Russia never really controlled the vast area that became Alaska since no more than several hundred Russians were present at most times.[11] The Russian America Company, similar to Britain's Hudson Bay Company, tried to manage both commercial and governmental issues with limited success. In 1857, Grand Duke Konstantin, the younger brother of Tsar Alexander II, proposed selling Russian America to the United States. Konstantin believed that the United States would eventually dominate North America and " ... these colonies bring us a very small profit and their loss to us would not be greatly felt ... "[12]

Baron Ferdinand von Wrangel had been the first president of the Russian America Company. He preferred not to sell either the company or Russian America but calculated market values as requested by the Romanov Court. Wrangel figured the Russian America Company was worth 7.5 million silver rubles and all of Russian America was worth 20 million silver rubles. Like any good cost estimator, he qualified his numbers, noting " ... it is impossible to require mathematical precision in appraisals of this sort ... "[13]

In the 1860s, a silver ruble exchanged for approximately 80 American cents, making the market value for the Russian America Company 6 million and the market value for all of Russian America 16 million in 1860 gold-backed dollars.[14] Wrangel did not mention petroleum in his evaluation even though Russian explorers had reported oil seeps in the Cook Inlet area as early as 1853. The sale stalled pending the outcomes of the American Civil War and an assassination plot.

April 1865 was a month Secretary of State William H. Seward would have preferred had never happened. First, he almost died when he tried to shut the door on his carriage after checking a problem with one of the wheels. The horses bolted, dragging him through downtown Washington, D.C. Nine days later, a co-conspirator of John Wilkes Booth stabbed Seward, recuperating in his sickbed at home, while Booth murdered President Abraham Lincoln watching a play at Ford's Theater. A metal brace Seward wore for the broken shoulder suffered in the near-fatal carriage accident protected his jugular during the assassination attempt.[15]

Two years after the near-death experiences, Seward reached an agreement for the purchase of Alaska. It had been a decade since Konstantin first proposed a sale. Some ridiculed the purchase, referring to Alaska as Icebergia, Walrussia, Seward's Icebox, and Seward's Folly. Despite the media and political noise, Congress handily approved the expenditure the next year. On a trip through the Pacific Northwest after leaving office, William Seward spoke in Sitka on August 12, 1869, about the rich natural resource potential of Alaska.[16] There was no mention of petroleum even though the oil age had been underway in both the United States and Russia for a decade or so.

The Federal Government and Alaska

Many Americans initially viewed Alaska as a wasteland. A land of extreme size, climate, and distance from just about anywhere, Alaska was also extremely unpopulated. Early critics wondered why Seward had bought a remote area one-fifth the size of continental America, home to 25 thousand indigenous peoples, a few hundred non-Natives, and probably covered with ice. For decades, the federal government neglected Alaska while it reconstructed the states torn apart by the Civil War. Explorers, prospectors, dropouts, and entrepreneurs filled the vacuum.

The American public received conflicting reports about Alaska's value from the beginning. In January 1870, H. H. McIntyre, special agent for the Treasury Department, concluded that based on economics, and not politics, the best course of action would be to abandon the place.[17] William H. Dall in a *Harper's New Monthly* article the same year, "Is Alaska a Paying Investment?" argued that the purchase would pay out in only fifteen years. Dall, an explorer and naturalist with the Western Union Telegraph expedition from 1866 to 1868, had kept extensive notes while surveying a potential communications link from North America to Russia across the Bering Strait.[18]

For decades after Seward's purchase, there was constant focus in politics and media on the value of resources extracted for the benefit of the nation versus the amount of federal subsidy required to maintain Alaska. Would Alaska ever pay out? General and soon-to-be President James Garfield recounted in a *Chicago Tribune* article that he had heard someone joke at a party that Seward had died years before he was buried because of the Alaska purchase. Garfield defended Seward's vision that the greatest achievements of man came from controlling the world's seas. He spoke of Seward's belief that the Atlantic was the ocean of the past and the purchase of Alaska assured America's dominance on the Pacific, the ocean of the future.[19]

By 1920, charts prepared for Congress showed that Alaska had not only paid for itself, it had already produced 150 times its purchase price. Alaska had exported over $1 billion (nominal) in resources at a cost to the United States of only one-fifth that.[20] Minerals and fish, mostly gold and salmon, made up 90 percent of the export value. The territory appeared to be a real estate bargain purchased during a Russian bear market for just over $12 per square mile. The Louisiana Purchase in 1803 had cost more than $18 per square mile. The Virgin Islands purchased in 1917 had run a staggering $190 thousand per square mile.[21]

Until statehood in 1959, the federal government owned nearly all of Alaska and managed virtually all resource development. A conservation movement in the early 1900s fostered by John Muir, Gifford Pinchot, and Theodore Roosevelt reserved large sections as national parks, forests, and wildlife refuges. These included the Tongass and Chugach National Forests in southeast Alaska and the Denali (Mt. McKinley) National Park in the interior.[22]

In 1912, the federal government granted territorial status to the District of Alaska yet retained land, mineral, fish, and wildlife rights. Alaskans paid federal income tax but could not vote for either their territorial governor or the president who made the appointment. It was a northwest version of taxation without representation.

Two years later, President Woodrow Wilson signed an act of Congress that authorized a nationalized railroad. The railroad targeted development of Alaska's interior. Secretary of the Interior Franklin Lane called Alaska the largest body of unused and neglected land in the United States. Lane commented about the lack of development, "The frank answer is that we did not realize until within a few years that it was worth developing."[23]

Alaska's remote location and an intricate web of red tape from forty federal bureaucracies complicated capital investment and resource development for decades. Territorial governors often returned to Washington to report to the nation about federal overmanagement. Thomas Christmas Riggs, a Princeton-educated engineer and governor of Alaska (1918–1921), argued against too much regulation by federal agencies.

In his 1920 annual report, he wrote, "In Canada, the founder of industry gets knighted; in Alaska, he very often gets indicted." Riggs challenged Congress to cut subsidies, to reduce the expanding federal bureaucracy, and to allow the territory to control its own resources. Riggs argued that Alaska should keep the profit generated from producing its resources rather than giving it to the U.S. Treasury. After fifteen years in Alaska, one pioneer commented that conservation was a guise to gather all of Alaska into an estate "managed by a devastating host of government underlings and worked by the citizens as lessees, licensees, and tenants. Alaska has literally been reserved to death."[24]

Today the federal government retains ownership and management of 60 percent of Alaska—more than any other state. The

The Great Land

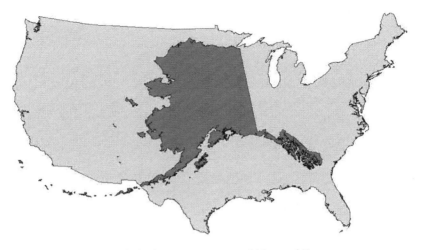

Courtesy of Alaska Department of Natural Resources.

state owns only 28 percent of its area, while Native corporations own almost 12 percent. Private ownership of land in Alaska is less than 1 percent.[25]

Two and one half times the size of Texas, Alaska accounts for 88 percent of America's national refuges and 65 percent of all its national parks.[26] Over time, the federal government has reserved most of Alaska, virtually designating it as a national multi-use park. Yet, despite the attention paid to preserving its environmental wonders, only one in nine adult Americans polled in 2006 has ever come anywhere near it, even for a visit. Most that came stayed on cruise ships in the southern part.[27]

Outsiders and Alaska

In 1885, Lt. Henry T. Allen, Sgt. Cady Robertson, and Pvt. Frederick Fickett of the U.S. Army set out from southeast Alaska. The patrol traveled up the Copper River to the Yukon River basin and west to the Bering Sea on a high speed, Alaskan version of Lewis and Clark. They covered 1,500 miles in twenty weeks. Their mission was to map the unknown interior and to assess any threats posed by Natives to future pioneers.

Several earlier attempts by Russian explorers to make part of the same trip had not ended well for the Russians. Along the way, Chief Nicolai of the Ahtna—Athabascans known to be territorial—helped Allen's expedition. Nicolai even revealed a secret outcropping of pure copper that Allen wrote about in a report he published a couple of years later.[28]

A discovery of gold in August 1896 near Dawson City, Yukon Territory, brought thousands of amateur prospectors to Canada and Alaska for a chance to get rich. Dreams of unlimited wealth just below the earth's surface lured the unemployed, disillusioned, and adventuresome to the Klondike. Promoters and newspapers in the Lower 48 kept the gold bubble inflated with stories of prospecting success. Dreams of unlimited wealth prolonged the mania.

New York journalist Tappan Adney brought some realism to the whole event in his book *The Klondike Stampede* (Harper and Brothers 1900). According to Adney, the Alaska Commercial Company of San Francisco and anyone else who sold services to prospectors made money. Almost every prospector went broke. Despite the media hullabaloo, Klondike output totaled barely $11 million at gold prices ranging from $16 to $17 per ounce.[29]

A pair of gold prospectors eating lunch in August 1900 noticed what appeared to be patch of green grass on the side of a mountain in southeast Alaska. It turned out to be a rich copper vein near Chief Nicolai's revelation to the Allen Expedition years earlier. Stephen Birch, a New York mining engineer and entrepreneur, accompanied a military expedition surveying the area for a road to connect the Yukon to the coast. After seeing the copper deposit for himself, he convinced investors to help him purchase the mineral claims.

J. P. Morgan financial and Guggenheim mining interests from New York decided to develop the rich copper deposits starting in 1906. To monetize copper ore found high in the Wrangell Mountains (named for Baron Wrangel although spelled with an extra *l*) required large amounts of capital, a market in the Lower 48, and a challenging transportation system. Using its own money, the Morgan/Guggenheim Syndicate carved a 195-mile railroad out of sheer rock canyons between the mines and the southeast coast near Cordova. Nearly half the distance consisted of bridges and trestles through areas subject to floods, hurricane-velocity winds, earthquakes, and avalanches. The syndicate also purchased a steamship line to haul construction materials in and to take copper out.[30]

Although the federal government generally neglected its northern possession, some in Congress became concerned that the "Morganheims" would monopolize and somehow "gobble up Alaska." Daniel Guggenheim framed the issue of Alaskan development in 1910: "Let the legislators make up their minds whether the government should build the railroads, or become a partner in the development by demanding royalties, or whether the government should simply throw the doors open to private capital. ... The thing to do is stop talking and to act."[31]

In 1915, the syndicate offered public participation through a stock offering, and a new Kennecott Copper Corporation managed the mines until the ore ran out in 1938. When the corporation shut down depleted mines after nearly three decades, fear grew among Alaskans that one day they could be stuck without any future source of revenue or jobs. Many blamed "outsiders" for taking their resources without regard for their future. The term *outsider* generally refers to large corporations and the federal government, but anything or anyone non-Alaskan qualifies.

In a 1941 address to the Alaskan legislature, territorial Governor Ernest Gruening complained that Kennecott Copper Corporation had taken $200 million worth of copper from Alaska, leaving only a hole in the ground and ghost towns. Gruening was from New York, a Harvard graduate, and a New Deal Democrat appointed by President Franklin Roosevelt. He urged more taxes on resources developed by outsiders and suggested placing some tax revenue in a savings plan for the future.[32]

Gruening's populist comments foretold the state's approach to oil taxation years later. It was true that Alaska needed to tax its resource base more to support government services. However, Gruening, like many in government today, viewed just one side of the balance sheet.

Gruening considered the $200 million worth of copper exported from Alaska as pure profit. He ignored the $25 million invested by the syndicate and corporation to build a railroad to the mines from the coast. Then there was the steamship line to get copper ore out of Alaska to the Lower 48 market. There was $50 million in wages for Alaskan jobs over decades, millions of dollars spent for supplies, and the time value of money.[33] The fact is that without outsider capital, risk-taking, and markets, Kennecott copper would have been and would still be worthless.

Decades later, oil companies would invest billions of dollars in Arctic infrastructure, an 800-mile Trans-Alaska Pipeline System, and ocean tankers to produce and transport another resource that also had no value without outsider capital and markets. Although oil has been a boom for the state of Alaska and an economic benefit for the nation, it has been a disappointing investment for oil companies. In part, this is due to the high taxes enacted to avoid a repeat, per Alaskan lore, of the Kennecott experience. Ignorance about the difference between gross revenue and net profit remains prevalent in federal and state governments today.

Alaskans Push for Statehood

Although territorial Alaskans generally favored resource development, they had little control over decisions made by the federal government or outside corporations. Gold mining and salmon constituted most of the economy leading up to World War II. Then the federal government shut down gold mines during the war, ending associated revenue and jobs for decades. To compound matters, Alaska recorded lower salmon catches from 1947 to 1976 during the recurrent ocean cooling cycle known as the Pacific Decadal Oscillation.[34]

Cold War defense spending dominated two-thirds of the economy from 1947 to 1957. When the territory of Alaska nearly went bankrupt in 1948, the legislature passed a personal income tax. It stayed in place for three decades until revenues from Prudhoe Bay oil production started to pour in. An entitlement culture has since developed based on living off Prudhoe Bay oil.

In the early 1950s, several oil companies started geological and geophysical studies on the Kenai Peninsula in southern Alaska. As the search for oil in southern Alaska ramped up, delegates gathered in Fairbanks to draft a constitution in preparation for possible statehood. In a convention speech, Bob Bartlett, territorial delegate to the U.S. Congress and a former gold miner, echoed Ernest Gruening's earlier warning about the dangers posed by outsiders after statehood:

> The first, and most obvious, is that of exploitation under the thin disguise of development; the taking of Alaska's mineral resources without leaving some reasonable return for the support of governmental services. ... The second danger is that outside interests. ... will attempt to acquire great areas of Alaska's public lands in order *not* to develop them.[35]

While Congress debated statehood, Richfield Oil Corporation (later merged with Atlantic Refining to form Atlantic Richfield Company or ARCO) discovered Alaska's first commercial oil on the Kenai Peninsula in 1957. Optimistic forecasts of potential oil revenue helped convince a majority in the U.S. Congress that Alaska could make it on its own as a state. In early May 1958, however, Rep. Howard W. Smith (D-Virginia) recorded common opposition to Alaskan statehood in a letter sent to House members. It stated, "Aside from many valid and compelling reasons why statehood should not be granted for Alaska, this bill provides for the greatest giveaway of potential natural resources in the history of our country." Smith saw Alaska as a warehouse of undeveloped resources that " … belong to all the people of the United States."[36] However, Alaskans saw the resources as *theirs* and for *their* benefit. The new state constitution said so.

Alaskans cherish their independence and see themselves as an "owner state." The concept is that the private sector finances resource development while government funds itself with royalty and tax revenue without taxing residents. Unlike most owners, however, the state and its residents do not share in the financial and operational risk of development other than wild swings in commodity prices.

Late Governor Walter J. Hickel envisioned the owner state as a hybrid of capitalism and socialism, a model for the former Soviet Union, and a new path to prosperity.[37] In reality, without investments, risk-taking, and markets provided by outsiders, there could be no owner state. Alaska will need to redefine this concept as oil production rapidly declines, leaving the owners nothing to tax.

Victims or Northern Sheiks

With statehood, Alaskans gained more control over some of the natural resources, but also gave up a portion of their federal subsidy. The Statehood Act provided a land grant and $30 million in transitional funds. However, the costs of running state government were higher than anticipated.

The first years as the 49th star on the American flag turned out to be even more challenging than territorial times. A financial crisis loomed. In 1960, Dr. George W. Rogers, an economist who consulted with the State Planning Commission noted, "If we don't develop our natural resources, we're sunk."[38]

When statehood was imminent, oil companies were making initial investments in geological and geophysical surveys above the Arctic Circle. Those exploration expenditures kept Alaska afloat after transitional funds ran out barely three years after statehood. By the end of 1967, the oil industry had invested $1.3 billion (nominal) in Alaska with little success. Then ARCO, an outsider, discovered Prudhoe Bay and saved the new state from an early financial collapse.

The state of Alaska funds its spending through oil exports. Like oil companies, it has no control over the price. Unlike state-controlled or nationalized oil in the Middle East, Alaska shares production profit with the federal government and the oil companies that finance and operate the developments. Just like Saudi Arabia, however, Alaska was impoverished before private companies found oil. The fear and insecurity that "Big Oil" might not leave Alaskans with a "fair share" of oil profits resulted in several tax increases even before there was any production in Prudhoe Bay.

In 1955, despite years of failed exploration and millions of dollars of capital losses by oil companies, the territorial legislature passed a 1 percent production tax on oil and gas.[39] In mid-August 1967, the Chena River flooded Fairbanks just before the winter freeze. Governor Hickel called a special session of the legislature to double the production tax on oil and gas to 2 percent to finance the rebuilding of Fairbanks. The flood disaster tax was supposed to be temporary. Nevertheless, after the discovery of Prudhoe Bay, the legislature doubled the production tax on oil and gas again to 4 percent, essentially making the flood tax permanent.

In 1970, environmental lawsuits and Native land claim disputes held back the start of Alaskan oil production. Oil companies absorbed daily losses from substantial early investments in production infrastructure and a trans-Alaska pipeline. This time, the legislature doubled the tax on future high-production wells to nearly 8 percent, the highest in the nation. They designed a new sliding scale tax of 3 to 8 percent, ostensibly to help the "little guy" by having lower-production-rate wells pay less tax. However, there have never been any "little guys" in Arctic Alaska, only "Big Oil."[40]

The oil companies had argued unsuccessfully to delay passage of another new tax until the start of production still seven years in the future. One industry representative made a comment in 1970 that still applies four decades later: "Too many of the legislators view Prudhoe as a big bonanza, not realizing that we are a high-risk industry—that Prudhoe is the exception, not the base case. They think we are [will be] making one heck of a lot of money, and they want their share."[41]

Alaska had high unemployment, a high cost of living, and a dependency on Washington for 60 percent of its revenue. A tax base from oil might provide financial independence. In what is now a familiar refrain, the federal government wanted more domestic sources to alleviate growing dependence on an unstable Middle East. Oil companies needed to pay out their past and future investment and to earn a profit for their shareholders. The profits trilemma encompasses three stakeholders: the state of Alaska, the federal government, and oil companies, each vying for a fair piece of the net pie; all destined to come away dissatisfied.

Before oil, Alaskans lived on the economic edge. Today they have grown accustomed to a tax-free society subsidized solely by oil money. In a state where oil revenue displaces a personal state income tax and *pays* citizens an annual check, there should be a mutually beneficial and strong partnership among oil companies and the state. Nevertheless, always simmering under the surface are territorial feelings that large corporate outsiders are extracting too much value without leaving Alaskans a fair share. This myth persists today and threatens any future development in Alaska.

The fear of not getting a fair share is a tenet of the state constitution, engrained in the psyche of the owner state, and the essence of the profits trilemma. The fear transcends political parties and has led to multiple tax increases on oil companies over the decades. As a result, government take through royalties and taxation in the so-called "red state" of Alaska has stealthily approached a level close to full government control or nationalization.

TWO

Looking for Prudhoe

Five hundred million years ago, most of the land mass on planet Earth sat close to the equator. During the Mesozoic Era (250 to 65 million years before present), spanning the Triassic, Jurassic, and Cretaceous Periods that saw dinosaurs, tectonic plates broke apart. They drifted like icebergs toward their current locations on the globe. The fifty-mile-thick plates floated on the outer molten mantle of the earth, moving at the speed of a growing human fingernail.[1]

As recently as 50 million years ago, the Arctic Ocean was still warm, teeming with water ferns and microscopic animals. There were no polar icecaps, temperatures everywhere were tropical, and climate change was minimal. As tectonic plates blocked warm ocean currents near the poles, icecaps began to form. Tropical Alaska transformed over time into an Arctic desert, while Saudi Arabia, near the equator, remained a hot one. Ocean basins formed along with the movement of plates. Rivers filled the basins with deposits of dead microorganisms. Under anaerobic conditions, dead matter retained its carbon-hydrogen bonding while successive sedimentary layers piled on. Over millions of years, overburden pressure from the layers created the right amount of heat in some places to cook organic material into petroleum.[2]

At 5:36 P.M., March 27, 1964, the North American tectonic plate slipped a little over the Pacific plate in a geologic process called *subduction*. During the next four minutes, the second-largest earthquake ever recorded released the energy equivalent of four trillion pounds of explosives and ruptured an area 500 by 150 miles. Near the epicenter, 14 miles under Prince William Sound, the seafloor rose 40 feet and ground levels dropped 8 feet.

In downtown Anchorage, 4th Avenue split down the middle and the façade on the new J.C. Penney building collapsed, killing two. The coastal neighborhood of Turnagain slid into Cook Inlet. Seismic sea waves caused most of 131 fatalities, some as far south as Oregon and California. The tsunamis obliterated Valdez and nearly all of Seward. Alaska has endured ten of the largest fifteen earthquakes in United States history. The biggest was the magnitude 9.2 Great Alaska Earthquake on Good Friday 1964.[3]

Plate tectonics explains how diverse deserts such as Alaska and Saudi Arabia contain oil. Both places are ancient tropical beaches, albeit with very different climates today. Dinosaurs are long gone; however, the formation of oil is ongoing as tectonic plates continue to drift. Geologists are using data from global positioning satellites and unmanned stations around the globe to track the movement and project the future locations of tectonic plates.

To a geologist, a 50-million-year projection is equivalent to making a five-day weather forecast. If one year is defined as Earth's 4.5-billion-year lifetime, 50 million years is equivalent to four geologic days. Four geologic days in the future, Los Angeles could be pushed northward adjacent to San Francisco, California.

Projections that are 250 million years out are more speculative. However, if tectonic plates continue to move as currently measured, California will sit next to Alaska. Los Angeles and Juneau will be twin cities.[4]

Elephants

There is a story about a geoscientist who was sampling rocks for traces of oil in the foothills of central Africa. He noticed that herds of wild elephants roaming the plains below him always seemed to gather at the same places. Plotting their herding locations gave him a break from the monotony of studying rocks.

After a few points, his plot began to form what resembled an elevation contour on a map. Since elephants are not climbers, he decided the center of his plot must be a crest. The crest was an *anticline* or upward fold in the earth with an impermeable outer layer and permeable rock at the core known to trap hydrocarbons. On a hunch, he convinced his company to drill an exploratory well. His intuition paid off when the well struck oil. *Elephant* has since become the term used to describe large oil discoveries.[5] Less than 1 percent of approximately 50 thousand oilfields ever discovered have been elephants containing a minimum of 500 million barrels of proven reserves. Proven reserves are amounts of petroleum recoverable given the technical and economic conditions present at any given time. Fewer than forty elephants in history have turned out to be supergiants with proven reserves of 5 billion barrels or more.[6]

The prolific Middle East is home to approximately thirty supergiants, while there have only been two in United States history. The first was the East Texas oilfield discovered during the Great Depression (1929–1939) and depleted by the early 1990s. By far the largest and only other supergiant in American history is Prudhoe Bay in Arctic Alaska. Confirmed as an oil discovery in early 1968, Prudhoe Bay is one of the twenty largest oilfields in the world, the largest in North American history, with proven reserves of nearly 14 billion barrels.[7]

Before Prudhoe

Ancient Romans called the substance that seeped from rocks *petroleum,* Latin for "rock oil." Natural seeps occur anywhere erosion or faults expose subsurface rock containing petroleum to the earth's surface. The La Brea Tar Pits in downtown Los Angeles, California, are natural seeps containing fossilized remains. The Athabasca Tar Sands in Alberta, Canada, are large accumulations of *bitumen* or oil bearing sands just beneath the earth's surface. Approximately 90 percent of all the oil ever formed within the earth has already seeped into the environment over hundreds of millions of years.[8]

Wherever petroleum seeps, indigenous peoples from the Middle East to Alaska have figured ways to incorporate it into their cultures and daily lives. Archaeologists have found that oil paved streets, embalmed bodies, greased wheels, and caulked vessels throughout recorded history, especially where it is the most prolific—the Middle East. Noah survived the flood in his large ark and Moses floated down the Nile in a tiny ark both sealed with pitch from oil seeps. Inupiat (Eskimo) residents along the Arctic coast cut blocks of oil-soaked tundra to burn as fuel for centuries before the discovery of Prudhoe Bay.

In 533 A.D., Byzantine General Belisarius unleashed several hundred greased, flaming pigs at a much larger army of enemy Vandals. The Vandals panicked. In Persia, on the west coast of the Caspian Sea, Zoroastrians built temples to honor eternal fires fueled by seeps representing their god, Ahura Mazda, now the name of an automobile. In the 13th century, Marco Polo reported observations of the burgeoning Caspian oil trade near what is now Baku, Azerbaijan, a large production center even today. In the 1700s, Russia controlled the Caspian Sea area and developed new distillation technologies to refine products from the large oil seeps. Peter the Great had "white" petroleum regularly shipped from Baku up the Volga River to his castle in the Russian capital city of St. Petersburg.[9]

Water well drillers in early America considered an oil discovery a failure and a financial loss. Soon, however, the entrepreneurial spirit emerged. In the mid-1800s, a Pittsburgh druggist bottled briny water laced with oil from his well in Pennsylvania and sold it as a cure-all he called "Rock Oil." An oilier version labeled "Seneca Oil," after the New York Indian tribe that endorsed its medicinal value, later became known as Snake Oil and the moniker for its salesmen.

While many took oil internally, scientists around the world worked on burning it. Canadian geologist Abraham Gesner refined the efforts of James Young of Scotland who had figured how to distill coal and oil shale into lamp oil. Gesner extracted a liquid from coal that he called *kerosene,* but it smoked and smelled which made it impractical for indoor use.

In 1857, a lamp-oil maker ran Seneca Oil through a distillation process similar to Gesner's and produced a much cleaner-burning fuel. All of sudden, crude oil was in demand, pooled oil seeps were exhausted, and water well drillers tried their hands at oil wells. In August 1859, oil officially became big business when the Pennsylvania Rock Oil Company, led by Edwin Drake, completed a well that flowed 20 barrels per day. The supply chain from drilling to markets fell into place and the commercial oil age began to take shape.[10]

The petroleum industry grew quickly after Drake's well struck oil at a depth of 69½ feet after a year of drilling. Other wells surrounding Drake's soon penetrated to depths beyond 400 feet. In 1968, the Prudhoe Bay discovery well found oil in the Arctic at about 9 thousand feet. In 2004, the progression to even more difficult oil continued with the "Jack" discovery by Chevron-Texaco in the deep waters of the Gulf of Mexico. That resource is 20 thousand feet beneath the Gulf's seafloor in 7 thousand feet of water.[11] In 2009, British Petroleum (BP) took it even deeper in the Gulf of Mexico to 35 thousand feet in 4 thousand feet of water with its "Tiber" prospect.[12]

In 1868, John D. Rockefeller established the Standard Oil Company of Pennsylvania and two years later the Standard Oil Company of Ohio. Rockefeller and associates, such as Henry M.

Flagler, decided to bring order to the new, chaotic industry by monopolizing it. Their objective was to make a product that would not smoke or explode. It needed to burn cleanly and be consistent in quality. In other words, they wanted "standard oil."[13] Rockefeller cornered the means of transportation, refining, and marketing rather than upstream exploration and production. The monopoly drove competitors out of business by undercutting their prices.

In 1875, while Rockefeller expanded Standard Oil, John Strong Newberry, chief geologist for the state of Ohio, claimed the end of the oil age.[14] By the turn of the century, however, the United States had produced its first billion barrels and a few thousand cars drove around on an ever-expanding network of roads. Newer oil states, such as Texas, parochially excluded Rockefeller and his Trust while several other states sued under anti-trust legislation. By 1911, fifty years after Drake drilled his famous well, the federal government dissolved the Standard Oil Trust, the original integrated oil company. Rockefeller went on to make even more money with his ownership in the pieces, the main one being Standard Oil of New Jersey (Exxon).

After World War I, oil shortages prompted David White, chief geologist of the United States Geological Survey (USGS), to warn that demand had overtaken supply. Without more discoveries, America would be out of oil this time by 1930.[15] Then came significant petroleum finds west of the Mississippi River primarily in Texas, California, Oklahoma, and Louisiana.

After a century of the oil age, the United States was the top-producing nation in the world. Oil and natural gas provided two-thirds of the country's energy needs, increasing to three-fourths by the early 1970s. From 1859 to 1959, 20 thousand independent oil companies had drilled well over one million exploration and development wells throughout America. The discoveries and gushers made all the news; however, the untold story was that two-thirds were dry holes and capital losses.[16]

By 1959, petroleum had become the primary source of power for the world's vast transportation network of planes, ships, trains, trucks and cars, and the foundation of the modern lifestyle. Even with fewer farmers, increased efficiency assured that a more populated America had a surplus of food. By 2010, only one in fifty Americans was a farmer, yet fewer farmers are able to produce more food with less land thanks to petroleum.[17]

Oil saved the whale and improved the nation's air quality by replacing wood and coal. In the 1967 Oscar-winning film, *The Graduate,* Mr. McGuire advised Benjamin Braddock, a recent college graduate with no plan for his future, to keep one word in mind—plastics—a petroleum byproduct. Mr. McGuire was right.

Early Alaska Exploration

In the late 1890s, gold prospectors came across what they described as a lake of oil big enough to supply the world. The oil dripped from rock and pooled along the Gulf of Alaska coastline.[18] The prospectors convinced a group of investors in Seattle, Washington, to secure land in the vicinity. They bought six miles of pipe from Pittsburgh, Pennsylvania steel mills to transport anticipated production to the coast for shipment out of Alaska.[19] The investors eventually leased their acreage to the Alaska Steam Coal and Petroleum Company that was looking for fuel to supply the British Navy. In 1902, the company drilled a well that at 300 feet resulted in "an immense oil gusher ... capped with great difficulty."[20]

Unfortunately, the pooled oil and the first gusher were just about all the recoverable oil there was. The rest had seeped away over millions of years, leaving only enough in the ground for a few low-producing wells. Several companies and investors scoured the area and much of the rest of southern Alaska. They spent hundreds of millions of dollars over the next sixty years trying to find commercial oil. The only success was a small oilfield and a refinery about fifty miles southeast of Cordova that intermittently produced a total of 154 thousand barrels from 1902 to 1934. Then the refinery burned down.[21]

For a short period after World War I, the normally self-sufficient United States had to import oil from Mexico. Marketers even restricted residents of California to two gallons of gasoline per stop when supplies became tight.[22] A lack of reserves in the growing post-war California market forced West Coast oil companies to look elsewhere for potential sources of supply, including the territory of Alaska. As early as the 1830s, explorers had reported petroleum seeps near Cape Simpson, east of Barrow and west of Prudhoe Bay.[23]

In July 1921, several expedition parties including Standard Oil of California (later Chevron) and General Petroleum Company (later Mobil) departed Nome on Alaska's west coast and headed 500 miles north toward Point Barrow. They were on the hunt for an elephant that could supply California markets. The *Oil, Paint, and Drug Reporter*, a trade journal, quoted geologists as predicting there could be one along the Arctic coast.

Even if they found one, however, it would be difficult to produce and transport the oil. A *New York Times* story reported that

> The problem of transportation looms up, should oil be found in commercial quantities, but it has been pointed out that if the expedition meets with success a pipe line could be laid from Point Barrow to Fairbanks, 450 miles, where connections could be made with the Government railroad. The region to be explored is reported to be flat country covered with about two feet of sand, beneath which the ground generally is frozen.[24]

During a trip to Washington D.C. in 1922, territorial Governor Scott Bone, originally from Indiana and appointed by

President Warren G. Harding, argued for incentives to encourage high-risk exploration and development of Alaska's Arctic oil potential:

> The time has come when honest capital must be encouraged to come into Alaska and develop the vast mineral resources. It cannot be expected that capitalists will be content with merely a nominal return on their money; for the risk of operating in a new country is always large. ... The indications are that abundant stores of petroleum exist. ... In these days when all the world is wondering where it will get fuel oil, this fuel is going to waste in Alaska. Of course, the development of these almost inaccessible oil resources cannot be accomplished unless large private capital be enlisted or the Government itself enters the field."[25]

If an elephant sat under the Arctic coast, only a large investment of capital by a corporation or government could unlock its potential. However, interest in Arctic Alaska soon faded when explorers made significant discoveries in Texas, Oklahoma, and California, much closer to consumers. The Arctic was just too expensive and too remote. Arctic oil would have to wait for a Middle East crisis several decades into the future.

In February 1923, President Harding designated 35 thousand square miles within the Arctic Circle, nearly 6 percent of Alaska, an area approximately the size of Indiana, as America's fourth Naval Petroleum Reserve. The federal government decided to reserve the area as a potential source of fuel for the U.S. Navy and possibly a future source of revenue for Alaskans. In 1976, the area became the National Petroleum Reserve–Alaska, NPR–Alaska, or NPR–A, when management transferred from the military to the Bureau of Land Management under the U.S.

Department of the Interior. In July 1923, after a visit to Alaska and just before his death, Harding outlined incentives necessary to attract capital investment:

> There are dreams of measureless oil resources in the most northerly section which are expressed in terms which sound more fabulous than real. Here is a discovery and a development demanding excessively large investment and a venture on the part of capital which the ordinarily justifiable restrictions utterly forbid. It is no project of hundreds of thousands of capital; it is the quest of tens of millions. Long distances to ports, the making of available ports, if the deposits are proven, demand that grants of leases be adequate to fair return for the big adventure. No native or individual enterprise is to be hoped for. To uncover the suspected riches there will need the lure of adequate return. We shall have to do whatever is necessary to encourage leasing and development or hold the vast treasure uncovered and futile ... [26]

Harding knew that developing Arctic oil would be more costly than anywhere else. However, even his extreme estimate at the time that development would need tens of millions in capital fell far short. It would take billions when the time finally came decades later.

Supergiants

In late 1929, a small, independent company named Pure found oil on the farm of Mrs. W. T. Jarman just east of Dallas. The widowed mother of nine told reporters she would not let the money go to her head except she might make a trip to Tyler for a new set of teeth.[27] A year later, a little farther east on Widow Daisy Miller Bradford's farm near Longview, a promoter, Columbus Marion "Dad" Joiner, originally from Alabama, found the East Texas oilfield.[28]

Joiner's discovery started an oil rush as gamblers, independents, and large companies converged to buy leases and to drill wells in the vicinity. Under the traditional "rule of capture," any oil found under a lease belonged to that lease even if the discovery was under another. Hundreds of operators scooped up land and drilled wells as quickly as possible to produce oil before others could take it from an adjacent land lease.[29]

During the first year, four more discoveries were made within a few miles of Joiner's. Initially thought to be separate oilfields, they all turned out to be part of one vast East Texas reservoir. By August 1931, production from East Texas approached one million barrels per day from 1,200 wells, well beyond world needs.

Operators ignored the law of supply and demand when they continued to produce more oil even as prices dropped. If anyone stopped producing, someone else would capture their portion. Because of the oversupply, prices eventually fell near ten cents a barrel. Everyone struggled to stay in business. The governor of Texas declared martial law and deployed troops to enforce the shutdown of wells in the hopes of avoiding a complete crash of the market.[30]

The East Texas experience led to conservation measures, improved reservoir management, and government oversight. From the 1930s through World War II, state and federal regulations restrained competition and maintained prices by prorating production among oil-producing states. The intent was to restrict supplies, to conserve resources, to maintain pricing, and to control the oil market.[31]

During a sixty-year life through 1992, more than 30 thousand wells produced 5.2 billion barrels from East Texas.[32] Through

2007, thanks to improved technology, the Prudhoe Bay oilfield had produced 11.5 billion barrels from just 2,500 wells, including approximately one thousand used to return natural gas and water produced with oil to the reservoir.[33]

Most oil companies curtailed their investments in American exploration during the Depression. Figuring the glut from East Texas would not last forever, a few of the larger companies gambled and headed overseas to explore the frontier Middle East. Chevron made a discovery in Saudi Arabia in 1938 that led to a partnership with Texaco, Exxon, and Mobil, and the formation of the Arabian American Oil Company (Aramco). At the time, only oil companies and a few geopolitical experts knew much about Saudi Arabia.[34]

Early in World War II, the federal government showed little interest in the Saudi Kingdom and its oil. As the war dragged on and the Nazis pressed their North African campaign toward the Suez Canal, Saudi oil suddenly took on national security implications for the United States. In 1943, President Franklin Roosevelt asked Secretary of the Interior Harold Ickes to send a team to the Persian Gulf area to evaluate its oil potential. Everett DeGolyer, the preeminent geoscientist in the country, led the effort and reported back to Washington what large oil companies there already knew. The center of gravity of the world's oil would soon shift permanently from the Americas to the Middle East and the Persian Gulf.

Secretary Ickes had unsuccessfully tried to nationalize the American oil industry before the war. Now he proposed that the federal government nationalize a major interest in the Aramco concession. Ickes got little support for his idea, especially from the free-market companies. After all, they had taken the financial and operational risk for more than a decade before the federal government even seemed to notice or care. As large Anglo-American companies developed Middle East oil resources, the American consumer enjoyed the best of both worlds. Energy was cheap and plentiful no matter where it came from.[35]

When the oil age celebrated its centennial anniversary in 1959, the United States was producing 7 million barrels from 583 thousand wells while importing another 2 million barrels daily.[36] Even though America led the world in oil production, an average domestic oil well produced only 12 barrels per day. Fifty years later, each of 500 thousand domestic oil wells produced on average fewer than 10 barrels per day.[37] On the other hand, 2 thousand wells in Saudi Arabia produced an average 5 thousand barrels per day each—about the same as 500 average U.S. wells.[38]

Many wonder how the United States came to rely so much on imported oil. Some complain that America has never had an energy policy. However, America's energy policy has always centered on keeping prices as low as possible for consumers. The federal government has tried to minimize "pain at the pump," regardless of the cost of production. Since domestic production has always been more costly than foreign production, Middle East oil produced by Anglo-American companies quickly became the preferred supply of choice.

Imports of cheaper oil were bound to rise and continue rising today despite nationalization, national security concerns, and mounting trade deficits. The only way to stem the tide is for consumers to pay for more costly domestic production and alternatives that are even more expensive. This always sounds good in theory, but paying more for energy and increasing "pain at the pump" is never popular.

The CANOL Project

In 1942, Japanese forces under Admiral Isoroku Yamamoto occupied the westernmost Aleutian Islands of Attu and Kiska. The American government feared an imminent attack on the Alaska mainland. In response, the U.S. Army Corps of Engineers hastily issued contracts to leading engineering firms to connect the Fort Norman oilfield in the Northwest Territories, Canada, to a new refinery at Whitehorse, Canada. The CANOL (Canadian

CANOL

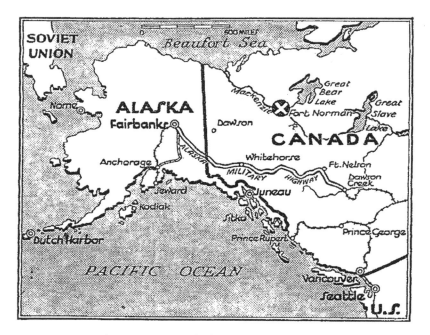

Source: New York Times, June 19, 1943.

Oil) Project included a fuel distribution system along the Alaskan Military Highway, now known as the Alcan, to supply Alaskan airfields. The supply route through Canada and Alaska was out of the path of Japanese submarines patrolling the Bering Sea and the Pacific Ocean.[39]

In 1789, North American explorer Alexander Mackenzie had found oil seeping along the banks of the large river now named for him near Fort Norman. In 1920, Imperial Oil (Exxon) discovered a reservoir in the same area. Imperial did not produce the well until local mining operations demanded a fuel source several years later. A recruiting poster in June 1942 warned prospective CANOL workers about the project. It was also a harbinger for future Alaskan workers:

THIS IS NO PICNIC

Working and living conditions on this job are as difficult as those encountered on any construction job ever done in the United States or foreign territory. Men hired for this job will be required to work and live under the most extreme conditions imaginable. Temperature will range from 90 degrees above zero to 70 degrees below zero. Men will have to fight swamps, rivers, ice and cold. Mosquitoes, flies and gnats will not only be annoying but will cause bodily harm. If you are not prepared to work under these and similar conditions **DO NOT APPLY**[40]

The CANOL Project was a wartime effort meant to strengthen North American defenses. Although it turned out to be minimally important, CANOL did result in the discovery of more oil at Norman Wells and renewed interest in further Arctic exploration. Geologists continued to believe that oil seeps throughout the region probably came from a large, untapped, parent source somewhere under the Arctic coast.

Toward the end of World War II, the U.S. Navy began drilling wells in the Naval Petroleum Reserve–Alaska about 180 miles southeast of Point Barrow to test for possible commercial oil. The federalized effort ended a decade later in 1953 with only minor shows of hydrocarbon. The largest discovery was an estimated 30 to 100 million barrels of noncommercial (not profitable) oil—nowhere near a supergiant. At the time, some experts thought that a 500-million-barrel Arctic resource might be sufficient to be commercial on its own.[41]

Despite the lack of oil discoveries, the logistical experience of the Navy and its contractors was a valuable result of the early exploration effort in NPR-A. The local air carrier, Wien Air Alaska, flew constant flights hauling supplies over the area blocked in by ice fifty weeks a year. Once a year in early August, the ice broke up for just a couple of weeks. A convoy of ships led by an icebreaker brought in the bulk of supplies and heavy equipment needed for the year ahead in a frantic race against nature. Crews unloaded the ships as quickly as possible before the icepack closed in for another year.[42]

Nationalization Forces Companies to the Arctic

Western companies controlled the technology and financial management of the world's oil through the 1950s. However, foreign governments, mainly in the Middle East, began increasing royalties and taxes on production, eventually leading to full nationalization. In 1960, a group of mostly Middle Eastern oil exporters banded together as a cartel to control supply and to obtain higher prices for their oil. Iran, Iraq, Kuwait, and Saudi Arabia along with Venezuela formed OPEC (Organization of Petroleum Exporting Countries). During the 1960s, eight other nations would join OPEC as it gained more control over the world's oil supply and pricing.[43]

During the 1950s and 1960s, companies restricted from nationalized regions focused more exploration effort in North America. They made large investments in unconventional technologies such as Canadian tar sands, oil shale, and clean coal as commercial alternatives to nationalized oil. One unique approach involved recovering oil from tar sands in Alberta, Canada, using a controlled underground nuclear blast.

The Atomic Energy Commission had detonated a nuclear device northwest of Las Vegas, Nevada, in 1957. After the Lawrence Radiation Laboratory at the University of California published the test results, Richfield Oil Corporation calculated that the same device at a depth of 1,400 feet could make recovery of crude oil from tar sands profitable.

Richfield was a California-based company that needed reserves and was looking to Canada and Alaska. Richfield applied to the Canadian government for permission to experiment with its theory. The Canadians were interested but an international moratorium on nuclear testing in 1960 scuttled plans.[44] Since no alternative energy sources could economically compete with petroleum, the search for conventional, domestic oil extended to more remote and more challenging areas including Arctic Alaska.

In 1958, the Bureau of Land Management opened to public leasing some NPR–A lands in the area of the Navy's earlier small discovery. On a hunt for elephants, BP geologic teams surveyed the foothills of the Brooks Range in Alaska. The area had similarities to the oil-rich geology of the Zagros Mountains of western Iran. BP had formed there in 1909 as the Anglo-Persian Oil Company.[45]

Iran had begun nationalizing its oil resources during the 1950s, gradually forcing BP toward Canada and then on to Alaska, where private investment was welcome. In Henry Longhurst's book, *Adventure in Oil: the Story of British Petroleum* (Sidgwick and Jackson 1959), a map inside the back cover shows the company's activities around the globe. The only place not shown as part of the world much less an area of petroleum activity is Alaska, the "Last Frontier."[46]

With its statehood land grant, Alaska selected acreage thought to be oil rich between the Colville and Canning Rivers along the Arctic coastal plain portion of the North Slope. In December 1964, Alaska held its first oil and gas lease sale that included North Slope tracts. Bidders included Atlantic, Richfield, and Sinclair (the three later formed ARCO), Humble (Exxon), BP, and SOCAL (Chevron). The 1965 sale offered the tract that held the yet undiscovered Prudhoe Bay reservoir, where Richfield would be the high bidder. A third sale in 1967 drew little interest as most companies had already given up on Arctic Alaska. The high cost, the extreme weather, and the lack of any exploration success for several years had taken a toll.

During the early 1960s, several companies had drilled eleven costly dry holes in northern Alaska. One of the most expensive was in 1966 when ARCO drilled a 2½-mile-deep dry hole sixty

Alaskan North Slope

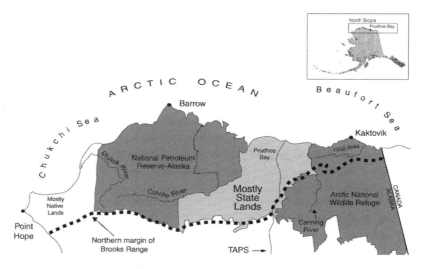

Source: GAO/RCED-99-191 Alaskan North Slope Oil.

miles south of the Arctic Ocean that cost $4.5 million or $29 million (2007). Even though ARCO had contracted to drill two wells, the company was out of patience, and worse than that, out of money. In a proverbial last roll of the dice, ARCO convinced Humble Oil and Refining Company (Exxon) to share the cost of one final Arctic well. Humble paid ARCO a bonus and agreed to finance 50 percent of the last well based on high permeability oil-stained sands from the area.

Thermometers broke and steel tools snapped as temperatures dipped to 70 degrees F. below zero. High winds dropped wind chill temperatures further to an equivalent 130 degrees F. below zero. Breathing itself was a chore as bodies struggled to process the temperature change from negative 130 to plus 98.6 degrees F. With those extreme conditions, a boiling cup of water tossed into the air instantly turned to frozen mist.

When natural gas came screaming out of the ground on December 27, 1967, the drillers said it sounded as if they were standing beside a roaring jet engine. After a few more weeks of painstaking work, they found oil deep beneath the frozen tundra and permafrost. Instead of a movie-style gusher, the oil came up the drill string under control.[47] The crew knew they had achieved something special even without the Hollywood drama. However, it was not yet clear that the discovery was big enough to be commercial.

On February 16, 1968, ARCO announced that the discovery well, Prudhoe Bay State No. 1, had found oil and gas zones in 200-million-year-old Triassic sandstone about 470 feet thick. The May 18 headline of the *Anchorage Daily Times* later proclaimed: "Arctic Oil Find Is Huge."[48] On June 25, 1968, ARCO announced that a second well seven miles to the southeast, Sag River State No. 1, encountered the same reservoir formation, confirming the astounding size of the discovery.[49] There was no natural gas cap this time, only oil. The good news—ARCO had likely found a supergiant. The bad news—it was over a mile and a half beneath the frozen tundra and 250 miles within the Arctic Circle.

THREE

Great Alaska Oil Rush

Alyeska experienced its first oil rush more than a century before the big discovery near Prudhoe Bay. Whale products had become popular in both America and Europe before the American War of Independence. Many New Englanders had turned to the sea to make a living. They sold whale oil, the preferred lamp fuel of the time, and *baleen*, keratin plates in the upper jaws of whales resembling combs used for filtering their food.

Baleen, similar to human hair and nails, is flexible when cut into thin strips. This characteristic made it useful for spokes, buggy whips, brush bristles, corset stays, and the fashion fad of the time, hoop skirts. Perfume makers used *ambergris,* a smelly, waxy substance regurgitated from colicky whales and found floating at sea, to make their unique fragrances last longer.[1]

New Englanders gradually dominated whaling around the world. When sperm whale harvests declined in the southern Pacific, the price of baleen rose. The law of supply and demand pushed whalers north, far from their markets, to find new sources.

Europeans had focused on whaling in the North Pacific for decades. Thomas Welcome Roys, while convalescing in Russia after a whaling accident, heard about a special whale found in northern waters.[2] In 1848, Captain Roys sailed his vessel *Superior* from Sag Harbor, Long Island, into the Bering Strait to explore for bowhead whale oil. After a month, he returned to Long Island with his ship's hold full. His success would support American whaling for the next fifty years.

Whaling peaked in the Bering Sea in 1852. That year, two hundred ships harvested $14 million worth, more than the Yukon gold rush would later yield. The take was so great that whalers feared they had over-harvested and decided not to come back for a few years.[3] Whaling vessels returned to the Bering Sea in 1858 until the final decline began in 1870.

In 1854, Roys retired from active whaling to research the Orca or *killer whale,* actually the world's largest dolphin.[4] He wrote how Orcas got their nickname. They clamp on to the tongues of other whales and pull them under water to drown them.

Thomas Roys spent the rest of his life designing harpoons and figuring how to extract more oil from discarded whale parts. After one last shot at seafaring, he contracted yellow fever. His crew left him ashore at Mazatlan, Mexico, where he died broke and mentally ill in 1876.

Petroleum saved the bowhead whale, but killed Edwin Drake. Seven years after his famous discovery at Titusville, Pennsylvania, he had already lost all his money as an oil trader. He lived destitute in Philadelphia, on a small stipend supplied by the state he had put on the oil map, until he died in 1880.[5]

A century after *Alyeska*'s oil rush, the Prudhoe Bay discovery vaulted Alaska onto center stage of the world petroleum scene. Reserves predictions by experts ramped up faster than spending plans by the state legislature. Alaska Governor Walter J. Hickel gazed out the window of his plane and mused that there could be 40 billion barrels of reserves below on the North Slope, 40 times more than he had surmised a year earlier.[6] According to Governor Hickel, Arctic Alaska held more recoverable oil than the rest of the country and nearly as much as all the rest of North America.

Commissioner Thomas Kelley of the Alaska Department of Natural Resources believed that even "the most ardent pessimist would be forced to agree that the geologic facts alone indicate Prudhoe Bay is only the first of several giant commercial fields to be discovered in this basin."[7] Charles S. Jones, former chairman of Richfield Oil Corporation commented that the size of the discovery was " ... certainly more than meeting the requirement that it be rich enough to justify the high expense of opening the Arctic Slope. The reserves on the North Slope may eventually equal all the presently known reserves of the lower forty-eight states."[8] An Anchorage hotel owner remarked, "It's the gold rush all over again, except this time it is oil, and the stampeders wear white shirts and carry seismic tools instead of picks and shovels."[9]

ARCO decided to get a third party assessment of its Arctic elephant. The company hired DeGolyer and MacNaughton, the most prestigious petroleum-consulting firm in the world, to perform an evaluation based on the first two wells and the available seismic data. On Thursday, July 18, 1968, ARCO reported the results to the public:

> In our opinion this important discovery could
> develop into a field with recoverable reserves of
> some five to ten billion barrels of oil, which would
> rate as one of the largest petroleum accumula-
> tions known to the world today.[10]

The consultants estimated the enormous find was 350 square miles in area, about twice the size of the East Texas field—clearly a supergiant. It would later prove to be *twice* that size. A *New York Times* story reported that if fantastic reserve figures as high as 5 billion barrels were true, the village of Umiat could soon be "knee deep in black gold."[11]

The fever spread to Wall Street as investors reacted to the initial assessment. Although Exxon stock opened for trading the day of the announcement, ARCO stock did not until the following Monday afternoon, when it closed higher by nearly $15 per share. ARCO stock, as low as $53 per share in January, hit a high of $130 at the end of November (including a two-for-one stock split in August).[12]

Francisco Parra, Venezuelan secretary general of OPEC, visited Wall Street in September 1968 to put a damper on some of the excitement. He reminded everyone where the future of world oil really was. He emphasized that Alaskan oil would be too expensive to export to Europe or Japan.

Parra told the financial community that North Slope oil would not be able to compete with the cheapest sources in the world. The Middle East held 62 percent of free-world oil reserves at the time. Parra also assured investors that there were no plans for the countries he represented to nationalize their oil interests—at least not yet.[13] As of 2009, National Oil Companies controlled more than 90 percent of the world's oil reserves—80 percent of the total controlled in the Middle East.

Michael Haider, chairman of Esso (Exxon), agreed: "One thing is certain, it won't be cheap oil. Drilling and developing will be relatively simple despite the harsh Arctic conditions, but transporting the oil will be the problem. It is very unlikely that it will be able to compete with Middle Eastern oil on the world markets."[14] Haider was correct about the transportation problem; however, nothing would be simple on the North Slope.

Which Way Out?

Transporting oil out of remote, Arctic Alaska to domestic markets thousands of miles away would prove to be a monumental challenge. Early brainstorm ideas included twelve-engine jumbo jets, railroad trains, and nuclear-powered submarines. Engineers quickly settled on three combinations of pipelines and/or tankers:

1. An 800-mile pipeline from the North Slope to Valdez in southern Alaska and then by tanker to refineries and markets such as Los Angeles.
2. A 1,500-mile pipeline from the North Slope to Edmonton, Alberta, in Canada connecting to existing or new pipelines that would carry the oil to markets in the Midwestern United States such as Chicago.
3. Via tanker from the Beaufort Sea, over the top of Canada, through a Northeast/Northwest Passage to the East Coast.[15]

In July 1968, helicopters packed with oil company employees were already scoping potential pipeline routes across Alaska and Canada. Each transportation alternative had its pros and cons. The companies considered a pipeline across Alaska as the least technically risky; but even after the oil got to Valdez it would still be thousands of miles from markets. The Canadian route put oil closer to the East Coast market that needed it most, but a longer pipeline would be more expensive and there could be unforeseen political issues going through a foreign country. The shipment of crude oil over the top of Canada via the Arctic Ocean could cut transportation costs; but it was untested and the Northwest Passage was frozen.

In early September 1969, the largest ship in the U.S. merchant fleet, the *S.S. Manhattan,* set out on a 4,500-mile journey from Pennsylvania toward Greenland and then west to Prudhoe Bay. Only ten vessels of any kind had ever traversed the Northwest Passage since 1906 when Roald Amundsen of Norway first did what explorers such as Cabot, Frobisher, Hudson, Baffin, Mackenzie, Parry, Franklin, and others had tried and failed at for more than four hundred years.[16] The oil companies, led by

S.S. *Manhattan's* Route

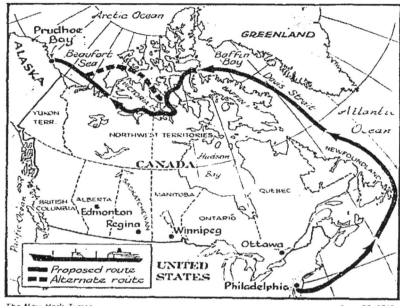

The New York Times   Aug. 25, 1969

Exxon, had spent $40 million to fit the *Manhattan* with a strengthened hull and icebreaking capability.[17]

  A small fleet of Canadian and U.S. icebreakers shadowed the tanker as it bashed as much ice as possible along the way to test its strength. Three weeks later, the ship dropped anchor thirty-five miles off Prudhoe Bay, where the continental shelf juts out about thirty miles. It was not able to get much closer since the bay is shallow. A helicopter flew a symbolic barrel of oil out to the *Manhattan* to complete the delivery before the tanker sailed back to Pennsylvania.[18]

  After the *Manhattan*'s voyage, the Canadian government extended its territorial waters from three to twelve miles offshore and declared the Northwest Passage as its own. Since then, Canada and the United States have agreed to disagree over sovereignty. The United States contends the passage is an international waterway open to all nations.[19]

It had been a difficult ocean voyage getting to Prudhoe Bay, and ice had badly damaged the *Manhattan*. It was clear to planners that building docks and loading facilities thirty miles from shore in the Beaufort Sea would be more difficult than building a pipeline. The most practical and cost-effective route appeared to be a trans-Alaska pipeline. The state of Alaska supported the all-Alaska option because it could gain construction jobs for the economy.

By late 1968, ARCO, BP, and Exxon began joint studies to design a pipeline system from Prudhoe Bay to Valdez on the southern coast of Alaska called TAPS. Overly optimistic oil executives with no Arctic experience told the media that TAPS would cost just $900 million. The estimate was based on a 500-thousand-barrel-per-day capacity pipeline—one-fourth that eventually installed.[20] It also assumed that most of the pipeline would be buried to prevent vandalism and reduce costs.

Oil companies had never designed an Arctic pipeline. They had not considered how a hot pipeline would behave when buried in frozen soil. The U.S. Department of the Interior wanted half the line elevated over sections of ground that could thaw and overstress buried pipe. That initial $900 million estimate for a smaller, buried pipeline has become a fixture of Alaskan lore since. Final costs for a larger pipeline that would handle higher flow rates, half of which was elevated, would turn out ten times greater.

In 1968, there were only four drilling rigs at Prudhoe Bay; just about everyone except ARCO and Exxon had given up on Alaska. BP continued to hold the lease adjacent to the one with the discovery. It spared no expense to get another rig to the North Slope as quickly as possible.

Exploration companies that had abandoned the Arctic rushed back. New ones piled in. Soon a dozen seismic crews working for as many companies pounded on their leases, listening for acoustic clues of potential subsurface structures that could hold oil.

In March 1969, BP announced that its drilling rig had found an extension of the Prudhoe Bay reservoir at its Put River No. 1

well. After drilling seven more wells, BP estimated as much as 4.8 billion barrels of recoverable Prudhoe Bay oil was under its lease.[21]

About the same time, Sinclair (later ARCO) discovered a shallower reservoir forty miles west of Prudhoe Bay. The shallower Kuparuk River oilfield would turn out to be a giant, one-fifth the size of Prudhoe Bay. ARCO also discovered a deeper, smaller formation called Lisburne while confirming the Prudhoe Bay discovery.

Alaska had suddenly become the hottest petroleum province in the Western Hemisphere. One confirmed supergiant, two speculative elephants, and myriad expert estimates promised unlimited potential.

Project management teams formed soon after confirmation of oil at Prudhoe Bay to determine the best way to handle the unprecedented program size and complexity. Extreme weather, low labor productivity, and a lack of existing support facilities on the North Slope made the cost of construction there prohibitive. Engineers already knew that it took at least five hours in the Arctic to perform the equivalent of one hour of work in the Lower 48.

The oil industry had no experience with permanent facilities in the extreme conditions. There were no standards for design, construction, and transportation of massive, enclosed facilities needed to process large volumes of oil and natural gas in the Arctic. With no precedent for figuring costs, project teams referred to their very rough order-of-magnitude cost estimates as "WAGs," aka wild-ass guesses.

In 1969, the skies between Fairbanks and Prudhoe Bay were jammed with aircraft shuttling cargo to and from airstrips built by the oil companies. There were hundreds of daily landings and takeoffs at Prudhoe Bay. A single C-130 Hercules air transport with a 15-ton payload needed over seventy round trips just to transport the parts for one drilling rig.[22]

In August, tugboats towed several barges loaded with 70 thousand tons of equipment and material to Prudhoe Bay during

Wien Air Alaska on the North Slope

the brief window through the ice. Cargo was transferred from larger seagoing barges to shallow draft barges in a process known as *lightering*. The companies constructed a dock to offload the shallow draft barges. By October 1969, a small refinery known as a Crude Oil Topping Unit began making Arctic-grade diesel, essentially kerosene or jet fuel, from Prudhoe Bay oil. Regular diesel turns to Jell-O at cold temperatures.

Hitching posts with electricity for engine block heaters would not be available for several years until installation of a Central Power Station. Vehicles ran around the clock in the cold; anything that stopped became an ice monument. Despite the harsh conditions, by the end of the year, a couple of dozen rigs had drilled more than thirty exploration wells in the frenzy.

Cold Fever Spreads to Washington

In a message to Congress in May 1948, President Harry Truman urged statehood for Alaska along with the development of

Alaskan oil to reduce the amount of foreign imports creeping into the country.[23] At the end of 1949, the United States was no longer energy independent. Few cared. Instead, the public and politicians, particularly in the highly populated East Coast, demanded more access to cheaper imports from Venezuela and the Middle East.

To preserve thousands of independent, domestic oil companies, the federal government tried to balance growing imports of foreign oil with more expensive domestic production. In 1957, the administration of President Dwight Eisenhower initiated a voluntary import quota system. However, oil companies that had risked large amounts of capital to develop substantial foreign holdings had little incentive to volunteer. In 1959, as cheaper imports continued to work their way into the country, President Eisenhower, although a supporter of free trade, reluctantly made the quota system mandatory. Eisenhower wanted to limit imports to no more than about 10 percent of domestic needs.[24]

In early 1969, oil imports continued to increase and approached 20 percent of demand despite a decade of quotas. In March, new President Richard M. Nixon commissioned the Cabinet Task Force on Oil Import Controls to review the Mandatory Oil Import Program and to recommend changes. Oil-consuming states favored removal of quotas on cheaper foreign oil to lower their energy costs. Domestic independents and oil-producing states wanted to retain import quotas since domestic sources were more expensive to develop and produce. Given the large discovery of Prudhoe Bay, the Cabinet Task Force also evaluated how Alaskan oil might affect import quotas and the world oil market.

Secretary of Labor George Shultz chaired the Cabinet Task Force staffed by the secretaries of State, Treasury, Defense, Interior, Commerce, and the director of the Office of Emergency Preparedness. As secretary of the Interior, former Alaska Governor Walter Hickel served as a member. Mid-study, Secretary Hickel, never shy about promoting development in Alaska, revised his North Slope reserves estimate upward for the second year in a row—from 40 to 100 billion barrels. Walter Levy, the recognized dean of oil consultants and economists in the country, enthusiastically declared the discovery of Prudhoe Bay meant that "The center of gravity of oil has begun to shift from the Middle East to the Arctic."[25]

There were hyperbolic predictions from nearly everyone except the oil companies. Swayed by the hype, Senators William Proxmire (D-Wisconsin), Thomas McIntyre (D-New Hampshire), and Edmund Muskie (D-Maine), each representing oil-consuming states, accused companies of hiding information from the Cabinet Task Force about the true size of Prudhoe Bay. In 1969, the senators asserted, " ... such information would seriously weaken any justification for continuing to force American consumers to pay exorbitant prices by keeping out inexpensive foreign oil."[26]

The senators wanted to import more oil from the Middle East because it was cheaper. In contrast, today, there are complaints about too much dependence on Middle Eastern oil. Despite the wild speculation and senatorial suspicions about the potential size of North Slope reserves, the Cabinet Task Force continued to use the high end of the published reserves range, 10 billion barrels, in its analysis.

In August 1969, after a six-month study, the Cabinet Task Force and Chairman Shultz recommended removing import quotas. They questioned the need to protect the domestic industry from foreign competition. One reason was their contention that Prudhoe Bay oil was cheap and more than competitive with Middle Eastern supplies anywhere in the United States, Japan, or Northern Europe. Oil companies were only then completing enough engineering to make initial cost estimates for an Arctic development. The Cabinet Task Force had decided to make its own assessments and to issue their report without consulting the industry. All of these initial "WAGs" by government and industry would prove far too low.

The Cabinet Task Force study reported that " ... a wellhead price has been calculated that will cover current and capital costs plus a 15 percent after-tax [rate of] return on all expenditures. ... It shows that on the stated assumptions (at least some of which appear conservative) the wellhead price of North Slope crude could be $0.36 per barrel."[27] Wellhead price determines the value of the oil before it enters the transportation system. The Task Force was not predicting that the wellhead price on the North Slope would be as low as $0.36 per barrel. Instead, in their estimation, that was the minimum price necessary to assure oil companies would earn a 15 percent after-tax rate of return.

The life of an investment is characterized as a series of annual net cash flows, which is cash in minus cash out for each year of the investment. The Cabinet Task Force used discounted cash flow (DCF) analysis to calculate a wellhead price. DCF is commonly used to rank projects for potential investment by considering the time value of money. The internal rate of return (IRR) is the discount rate at which the net present value of the annual net cash flows adjusted for inflation equals zero. A project is considered for investment if its projected IRR is better than other projects, other investments, or just holding cash.

The discount rate often used to benchmark prospective projects is the average cost of capital, sometimes called a *hurdle rate*. Companies use a combination of debt and equity as sources of capital to fund their investments in projects. One early analysis determined the average cost of debt and equity capital for a Prudhoe Bay development at just over 13 percent. From 1968 data presented in testimony to the Senate Subcommittee on Antitrust and Monopoly, the average after-tax rate of return on oil investments in the Lower 48 was also 13 percent. Due to the higher risks involved, the Cabinet Task Force set the minimum after-tax rate of return or IRR higher for Prudhoe Bay development at 15 percent to encourage oil companies to invest in Alaska's Arctic.[28]

Companies hope to earn more than the hurdle rate to add value and to provide capital to fund future investments. Consistent with financial theory, the expected rate of return varies with relative risk. In other words, the higher the risk undertaken, the greater the expected reward.

In mid-1969, the quoted delivery price for domestic oil along the Gulf Coast was $3.50 per barrel. Foreign oil was half that delivered to the East Coast. According to the Cabinet Task Force, North Slope oil could easily compete with foreign oil.

The study projected delivered prices of North Slope crude as $0.76 per barrel to Northern Europe, $0.96 to Japan, $1.11 to Los Angeles, $1.36 to Chicago, and $1.81 to the U.S. East Coast via the Panama Canal. The difference between delivered and well-head prices is the cost of transportation by pipeline and ocean tanker to each location. For example, the estimated cost of transportation from the wellhead to Los Angeles refineries was $0.75 per barrel ($1.11 minus $0.36) in the Task Force analysis.

The White House Cabinet and government economic experts told the public that the United States was swimming in virtually unlimited, cheap Alaskan crude. Alaska North Slope oil could be America's answer to the Middle East and an end to oil imports forever. The study results flew in the collective face of the companies that claimed North Slope oil would be the most expensive in the world. The Cabinet Task Force even challenged ARCO, BP, and Exxon to disprove their study's "conservative estimates" and to "provide better data or a more persuasive analysis."[29]

In August 1969, the Cabinet Task Force reported its results in the media. According to the study, any market price at $1.11 per barrel (nominal) at Los Angeles (just over $6 per barrel in 2007 dollars) would bring tremendous profits. According to a *New York Times* story, the Cabinet study had highlighted serious concerns in the country about pollution, protectionism, taxes, and high oil company profits.[30]

The White House Cabinet Task Force study and media reports would prove to be seriously inaccurate. An updated federal study completed just two months before the start of production did, in fact, contradict their results. The Federal Energy Administration (FEA) found that the market price at Los Angeles needed to average between $13 and $14 per barrel (nominal) or approximately $50 per barrel (2007) to provide a 15 percent IRR to oil companies for producing Prudhoe Bay. Robert O. Anderson, then chairman of ARCO, later wrote about the Cabinet Task Force, "It is difficult to believe that a supposedly competent and well-informed group could have so seriously underestimated costs and thereby misled the public on an issue of this magnitude."[31]

Many economists believed that removing import quotas and adding an import tax instead would drive down prices for domestic oil, while imports of less expensive sources would increase even more.[32] One hundred congressional representatives sent President Nixon a letter denouncing the potential removal of import controls as a threat to the domestic oil industry and national security.

President Nixon rejected the majority recommendation of his Cabinet. Instead, he decided to retain the quotas until just after the energy crisis of 1973.[33] After the discovery of Prudhoe Bay, it was as clear to ARCO, BP, and Exxon as it had been to President Warren Harding that North Slope oil would be expensive and difficult to produce. Inexplicably, President Nixon's White House Cabinet and expert economists working for the federal government had freely publicized conflicting views that Alaska would be an oil company bonanza.

Peak Prudhoe Mania

In September 1969, just before the first major North Slope lease sale, an economic presentation at the Alaska Science Conference in Fairbanks sponsored by the University of Alaska shocked participants. A resources economist with the university's Institute of Social and Economic Research (ISER) outdid even White House Cabinet Task Force economists. He claimed the present value of North Slope acreage was so large that the oil companies did not have the combined financial assets to bid its true worth.

According to the ISER economist, oil companies would achieve a 43 percent rate of return over a twenty-year life of Prudhoe Bay at then current tax rates. A *New York Times* story reported that the economist further stunned the audience when he claimed that the state should take 85 to 90 percent of the gross wellhead value. He contended that oil companies would still earn greater than a 10 percent rate of return.[34] In reality, with billions forecasted to be spent before production could begin, given his assumptions, companies would have to pay the state more than the oil was worth to produce it. The speculative bubble continued to inflate.

On September 10, 1969, fifty companies convened in an Anchorage auditorium to participate in what *Time* magazine called the richest auction in history. They had come to bid for leases on state-owned coastal land near the Prudhoe discovery. A queue began forming at three in the morning. Alaska's Governor Keith Miller called the auction a "rendezvous with our dreams."[35]

Before the day was over, fifteen companies had paid over $900 million, about $5 billion (2007) for mineral leases on the North Slope. A half million acres of leases returned an average bid per acre of over $2 thousand. One tract brought in over $28 thousand an acre. Earlier lease sales in 1965, including the one with the Prudhoe Bay discovery, had averaged only $13 to $15 per acre. The mania was in full bloom.

An editorial in the Anchorage newspaper afterward praised Alaska's Commissioner of Natural Resources: "Kelly got rid of a lot of caribou pasture at some pretty high prices. He played a tremendous poker game and won for the state all the way."[36] Lease sale returns earned $200 thousand a day in interest while the legislature figured out how to spend nine times the state budget for fiscal year 1968.[37]

After the big lease sale, experts began predicting that there could be 50 billion barrels of recoverable oil on the North Slope. According to federal and state governments and their consultants, everything about oil in Alaska seemed too good to be true.

Alaska, resources rich and cash poor, had little to show for a domestic economy before the Prudhoe Bay discovery. At statehood, Alaska's cost of living was 50 percent higher than the rest of the country. Sixty percent owned by the federal government, Alaska depended on federal subsidies for 6 of every 10 dollars. Education was a top priority. Poverty existed in rural areas inhabited mainly by the state's 50 thousand Native peoples, about 20 percent of the population.

In late 1969, more than one hundred select Alaskans participated in four sessions facilitated by the Brookings Institution to grapple with questions about financing their future. The results called for more spending on issues affecting the state at the time. That meant education, health, and welfare, and the development of natural resources in the best interests of Alaska. About two-thirds of the $900 million from the lease sale wound up going to education over the next few years.[38]

Many non-Native Alaskans had come north to escape big city growth and to live an uncomplicated, frontier life. Mostly outsiders from Texas and Oklahoma staffed the North Slope. The large military population temporarily stationed in the state had little interest in long-term oil development issues. The fishing industry generally did not care about the North Slope as long as the development had no effect on the annual harvest. The last things most Alaskans wanted to worry about were big government, big taxes, big issues, and big responsibilities. One Anchorage businessman summed it up commenting, "Oh, it's exciting and challenging, I guess. But sometimes I sort of wish that Prudhoe Bay well had been a dry hole."[39]

It had taken almost a decade from the first investments in exploration surveys on the central North Slope until the discovery of oil near Prudhoe Bay. After years of dry holes and the eleventh-hour find, companies hurried to pay out their early investment and to return a profit to shareholders. At first, oil executives announced that production could start in three or four years, as early as 1972.[40] They were in for a rude awakening.

Although the Great Alaska Oil Rush proceeded throughout 1969, there would be no production for nearly another decade. Everything about oil and the environment was about to change forever. Soon, North Slope oil companies would also almost wish that Prudhoe Bay, the largest reservoir in North American history, had been a dry hole.

The federal government had told the public that Arctic oil was cheap and inexhaustible. However, at the European Institutional Investor Conference in London in December 1969, Thornton Bradshaw, President of ARCO, noted that 10 billion barrels of reserves from Prudhoe Bay was worth just two years of supply for the country. Bradshaw commented, "Prudhoe Bay may be the answer to an oil company's dream—it surely is to Atlantic Richfield's—but it is not the answer to a nation's needs."[41] Oil executives attending the conference agreed that the international oil industry would remain focused on the tension-ridden Middle East.

A huge disconnect existed among industry, the federal government, and economists regarding the cost and potential benefits of Alaskan oil. The presumed answer to an oil company's dream would soon morph into a financial nightmare and a multiyear national ordeal.

FOUR

Long Ordeal

At the start of the oil age, just one in five Americans lived in a city. By 1970, almost three-quarters had packed into congested metropolitan areas. Federal regulations had been largely ineffective in slowing down the pace of industrial discharges during the twentieth century. As a result, the consumer society fueled by cheap energy was starting to experience pollution. As population density increased, a firestorm of environmental outrage awaited an ignition source.

For millions of years, petroleum has seeped into the Santa Barbara Channel through the cracked-eggshell geology of the California seafloor. Throughout recorded history, indigenous Chumash Indians had collected tar found on West Coast beaches to waterproof their canoes and baskets.[1] In 1896, seeps enticed operators to drill angled wells from piers along the coast to access pockets of oil in the shallow waters just offshore. Sixty years later, California had its first offshore platform, Hazel, in just less than 200 feet of water.[2]

During January 1969, five drilling rigs were operating in federal waters six miles off the California coast near Santa Barbara. On one, operated by Unocal Corporation, the crew was extracting pipe from a fifth well drilled from the platform when they experienced a natural gas *blowout*. The weight of mud in the drill pipe was not sufficient to counterbalance the natural pressure of the reservoir.

Drilling mud is a mixture of clay, water, and chemical additives pumped down hole through the drill pipe. It cools the rotating drill bit, carries rock cuttings to the surface, and keeps the hole from collapsing until casing is set. Casing is steel pipe cemented into the well bore to seal off reservoir fluids and to permanently prevent the hole from caving in.

The blowout preventer, a system of large valves on the wellhead, rammed shut and sheared the drill stem as designed. Nevertheless, high-pressure natural gas forced itself through existing fissures in the seafloor. Soon an oil slick formed that coated miles of coastline.

It took eleven days of pumping cement down hole to seal the leak and four months to clean up approximately 80 thousand barrels and several miles of beach. The well had discovered oil and a lot of emotion.[3] The sight of a slick and thousands of dead birds along the California coastline galvanized public sentiment against offshore drilling.

Investigators later determined the cause of the blowout was inadequate casing design even though Unocal had followed applicable federal regulations. The rupture would not have happened had the company followed more stringent state of California regulations specific to offshore operations closer to shore. Regulations in state waters required thicker-walled casing that extended deeper.

Newly confirmed Secretary of the Interior Walter Hickel faced a baptism under fire. Washington D.C. columnist Drew Pearson portrayed him as an oilman in the pockets of North Slope oil companies. Clearly, Pearson did not understand Hickel's quasi-socialistic concept for resource development in the owner state.

Secretary Hickel issued an executive order stopping offshore operations throughout the country until new federal regulations were drafted and in place. Unocal took responsibility for the cleanup and the cost, but the spill was a public relations disaster.

Unintentional releases of large volumes of petroleum can overwhelm an ecosystem but they are the exception. Most oil that enters oceans does not come from exploration, production, or spills. Nearly two-thirds of the petroleum in North American waters comes from natural seeps. Most of the tar left on feet after visits to local beaches comes from seeps.[4]

In 1982, ARCO set two steel pyramids weighing 350 tons each in 220 feet of water just north of Santa Barbara to collect oil and gas from seeps in the area.[5] Research, based in part on the volumes collected by the pyramids, found that 150 thousand barrels of oil seeps naturally along the southern California coastline every year. That means the equivalent of three *Exxon Valdez* spills naturally oozes into ocean waters along California's coast every five years.

Total oil lost because of offshore development since the Santa Barbara spill averages less than 500 barrels per year. Even so, California has not issued an offshore lease for oil exploration since. In the platform-intensive Gulf of Mexico, natural seepage exceeds one million barrels annually, which is equivalent to more than four *Exxon Valdez* spills every year.[6]

In 1969, with plenty of cheap oil available, many wondered why the country would risk damage to its most pristine areas just so companies could earn perceived "exorbitant profits." A national Earth Day merged into the anti-war movement on college campuses that spring. President Nixon commented:

> It is sad that it was necessary that Santa Barbara
> should be the example that had to bring it to
> the attention of the American people. What is
> involved is the use of our resources of the sea and
> of the land in a more effective way and with
> more concern for preserving the beauty and the

Prudhoe Bay Operations Center (Summer 1976)

natural resources that are so important to any
kind of society that we want for the future. The
Santa Barbara incident has frankly touched the
conscience of the American people.[7]

President Nixon signed the Endangered Species Act in 1969
and the National Environmental Protection Act (NEPA) on January 1, 1970. Emotions about a pipeline across pristine Alaska
escalated. There were calls to slow down or even halt the oil rush.
The Santa Barbara spill turned Alaska into what ecologist Barry
Commoner called "a living microcosm of the whole environmental issue."[8]

An overwhelming majority of Alaskans favored oil development. Outsiders, figuring they knew better, however, decided to
protect Alaska's land, people, and wildlife. Federal right-of-way
permits for TAPS had already been filed during summer 1969.
However, environmental groups countered with lawsuits to halt
construction permits in April 1970. Although the Prudhoe Bay
oilfield is on state-owned land, the pipeline route needed to

cross several hundred miles of federal land. Under NEPA, a federal judge stopped construction until companies developed a detailed plan required by the new regulations, an Environmental Impact Statement.

Environmental groups saw the "Last Frontier" as the conservation battleground of the century. Ecologists portrayed the Arctic as a fragile ecosystem with little biodiversity. Interior Secretary Walter Hickel commented, "It used to be the hostile, frozen north; now it's the goddamn, fragile tundra."[9]

Hurry Up and Wait

By the end of 1970, the only urgency to produce Arctic oil existed with the state of Alaska, which needed revenue and jobs, and in varying degrees with ARCO, BP, and Exxon. ARCO needed reserves most, while much larger Exxon was ambivalent. The Alaska oil rush was over as quickly as it started. The long wait to get federal permits needed to build TAPS had begun.

Exploration companies decided not to drill any more wells on the North Slope. Investment in high risk, expensive exploration, with no way on the horizon to transport oil out of Alaska, made no economic sense. During summer 1970, a fleet of sixty tugs and barges delivered 185 thousand tons of equipment and facilities for Prudhoe Bay infrastructure—all in vain.[10]

By then, more than half of the 29 drilling rigs flown in pieces to the North Slope were idled and only ten or so wells were still underway. Millions of dollars' worth of pipe ordered from Japan stacked up. It became apparent that there would be a long delay for a pipeline across Alaska.

Construction of a "haul road" along the northern part of the pipeline route came to a halt. Workers were paid to wait around for months at ten construction camps between the Yukon River and Prudhoe Bay before they were demobilized.

The oil companies used the delay to start the process of developing a unitization plan. Even the largest oil companies do not have the financial resources or the desire to assume the risk of mega-scale developments alone. Companies often organize into units and joint ventures in order to share revenues, costs, and risks according to their individual ownership percentages. The unitization plan would formally divide the ownership of billions of barrels of oil and trillions of cubic feet of natural gas on the North Slope.

A unit approach also saves money and maximizes petroleum recovery. Unitization minimizes environmental impacts that would result if each company built individual facilities and pipelines as happened under the "rule of capture" at East Texas during the 1930s. BP became the unit operator for development of the western half of the North Slope while ARCO became the operator on the eastern half.

Under a joint venture pipeline agreement, each TAPS owner got sole possession of a portion of the large pipeline as if each owned an individual pipeline. ARCO, BP, and Exxon together controlled about 95 percent of both production and pipeline transportation. Several minority owners shared interests in the remaining 5 percent of either production and/or TAPS.

Project management teams returned to the drawing boards to improve Arctic design concepts. ARCO decided to scrap two undersized separation facilities shipped from Texas during the 1970 sealift. The project team started over and hired a new managing contractor more accustomed to large projects, Parsons Corporation in California.

The overall North Slope development plan began to take shape. To keep frozen tundra insulated and undamaged, the design called for gravel well pads and roads from five to seven feet thick. The companies would directionally drill wells from the pads to reduce miles of roadway and associated environmental impacts. Individually housed wellheads would allow year-round access for maintenance even during the worst days of winter. ARCO and BP also decided to use centralized power generation and natural gas handling rather than installing separate facilities on each side of the field.

Despite the design activity in California, the oil rush in Alaska ground to a halt. Unemployment reached 13 percent statewide and 25 percent in Fairbanks. Information booths at Lower 48 airports warned job seekers not to come north since there was no work in sight.[11] There would be no trans-Alaska pipeline, no oil production, and no return on investment for oil companies for several more years.

This Land Is My Land

After statehood in 1959, some of the various Native groups pressed ancestral claims on land. When Alaska selected the area around Prudhoe Bay as part of its statehood land grant, the Arctic Slope Native Association filed suit that the Inupiat (Eskimo) owned the entire North Slope. In 1966, the Alaska Federation of Natives (AFN) formed in Anchorage to lobby the issue.

Later that year, Secretary of the Interior Stewart Udall stopped all land transfers pending the settlement of aboriginal claims. Oil development could not proceed until the federal government and Alaska's Natives reached a settlement. By 1970, the AFN had claimed 90 percent of the state as an opening position in negotiations with federal and state governments.

There was progress on December 18, 1971, when President Nixon signed the Alaska Native Settlement Claims Act (ANSCA). Rather than creating reservations under the Bureau of Indian Affairs, ANSCA organized Alaska's Natives into thirteen regional corporations that became owners of land and mineral rights in the vicinities of 200 or so villages. One of the thirteen corporations covers Natives living outside Alaska's borders. Native corporations received in total 12 percent of Alaska's land and $1 billion in exchange for no future land claims. One half of the cash settlement would come from the state's oil royalty and the other half from federal appropriations over eleven years.

Every Alaskan at least one-fourth Native qualified as a shareholder at settlement. That included 75 thousand Aleuts, Eskimos, and Indians, each entitled to dividends and voting rights within their respective corporations. ANSCA assimilated Alaska's Natives into a capitalist economy with a socialist twist—each regional corporation shares 70 percent of its revenues with the other twelve.[12]

ANSCA was the largest land claims settlement in American history. President Nixon declared, "This is a milestone in Alaska's history and in the way our government deals with Native and Indian peoples."[13] Even with land claims settled, it would take two more years and an energy crisis before construction of a trans-Alaska pipeline would begin.

The End of Cheap, Unlimited Oil

In 1965, a high-level federal energy study group decided that the United States needed to use more of its own oil as soon as possible. They concluded, "The nation will regret that it did not make greater use of these stocks when they were still precious."[14] According to the study, unless the United States used its own oil quickly, there could be so much cheap Middle East oil on the market in the future that domestic supplies would have little value.

After the discovery of Arctic oil, Morris Adelman, professor of economics at the Massachusetts Institute of Technology, consulted with President Nixon's White House Cabinet Task Force. He wrote, "Because Prudhoe Bay oil is very cheap, there has been a headlong rush into the North Slope. ... *The very low development-production cost is the only explanation* [Adelman's italics] ... the oil companies do not want oil for oil's sake; there is more in the lower forty-eight than they will ever use; what they want is cheap oil."[15] In Professor Adelman's opinion, the only reason companies wanted to develop the North Slope was that it was cheap to produce and more profitable than other sources.

In May 1970, a bulldozer digging trenches for telephone cables in Syria damaged the Trans-Arabian Pipeline connecting Saudi Arabian oilfields with the Mediterranean Port of Sidon in

Lebanon. Syria refused to allow a repair for nine months until receiving higher pipeline fees. Around the same time, Libya decided to cut back on its oil production.[16]

For the first time ever, imports to the eastern coast of the U.S. suddenly cost more than domestic oil. Politicians and consumers in oil-consuming states had always demanded cheaper Middle Eastern imports over more expensive domestic production. Now, they began to worry about their addiction to non-domestic sources.

Preeminent economist Walter J. Levy reversed himself after proclaiming Alaska a new Middle East just a year earlier. As problems between Arab countries and Israel escalated, Levy noted, "These are terrible, dangerous, and difficult times."[17] The Alaska legislature had hired Levy's consulting firm to advise them on petroleum policy. Turning on a dime, Levy advised the legislators that Alaska was small in the world picture, "so move slowly and cautiously."[18]

By March 1971, to make up for the reduced foreign supply, the Texas Railroad Commission allowed wells in Texas to produce full out for the first time since 1948. However, the wells no longer responded with more production as they always had before. Suddenly, there was a lack of sufficient domestic supply to make up the difference. President Nixon addressed the nation with a new energy paradigm in June 1971:

> For most of our history, a plentiful supply of
> energy is something the American people have
> taken very much for granted. In the past twenty
> years alone, we have been able to double our
> consumption of energy without exhausting the
> supply. But the assumption that sufficient energy
> will always be readily available has been brought
> sharply into question within the last year.[19]

It would be clearer in a few years that Lower 48 oil production had begun declining in 1970. The shortage had not been contrived by oil companies as many politicians, activists, and pundits had charged. With less domestic supply available, imports into the U.S. increased. The increase permanently erased President Eisenhower's original 10 percent import line in the sand.

U.S. Oil Production

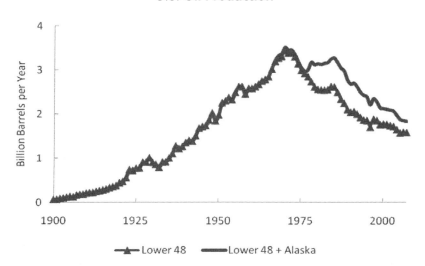

Data Source: Energy Information Agency (EIA).

M. King Hubbert, a Shell Oil Company geologist, developed a theory in 1956 that predicted a peak in Lower 48 production rates based on cumulative production. Peak oil advocates apply Hubbert's concept to worldwide production. An academic debate rages regarding the validity of Hubbert's Peak or the point of highest production. The theory is useful but ignores the two most important factors regarding petroleum production—oil price and government. Despite improved petroleum technology, the only way to find oil is to drill for it. Operators target large structures first for development if commercial. Other fields may be nonconventional, off-limits politically, smaller, or more expensive to produce. Oil prices must remain high for long periods to make them commercially attractive. In any case, domestic American production peaked in 1970 just as Hubbert predicted.

The North Slope was able to reverse the decline for its first few years of production. By the end of 2007, however, United States annual oil production had fallen to 1.86 billion barrels, or about 5 million barrels per day. That was the lowest since 1949, the last year of American energy independence.[20]

It Takes a Crisis

Since World War II, the American consumer had enjoyed cheap, abundant domestic supplies and even cheaper imports provided by large, Anglo-American oil companies—"Big Oil." Oil prices had trended down in real dollars from 1950 to 1970. Supply had always been greater than demand thanks to spare capacity from domestic oilfields, particularly in Texas. Unknown to most of the public, however, everything to do with oil had been changing. The shift of the center of gravity of oil to the Middle East was underway just as predicted during the Franklin Roosevelt administration three decades earlier.

In October 1973, oil prices doubled in the wake of the Yom Kippur War. Middle East suppliers refused to ship oil directly to countries that supported Israel—especially the United States.

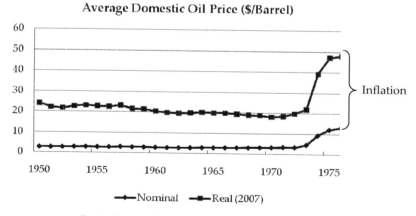

Data Source: Energy Information Agency (EIA).

OPEC used its newfound strength to curtail production and to increase prices.

Before year end, oil prices doubled again. The difference between supply and demand became apparent in the world system. Western Europe and Japan got most of their oil supply from the Middle East. America, on the other hand, had access to some domestic sources to help bridge the supply gap. Even so, gasoline lines soon appeared. A frustrated public, as always, turned to the federal government to "do something." The Nixon administration, trying in vain to manage soaring inflation, printed gasoline rationing coupons as a contingency but never used them.[21]

During summer 1973, Vice President Spiro Agnew had to break a 49–49 vote in the U.S. Senate to prevent further environmental challenges to the construction of TAPS. Some senators still favored a more expensive pipeline route across Canada to supply major East Coast metropolitan centers. It was no longer popular to import foreign oil. However, that longer pipeline would have been a financial disaster for all stakeholders. In late 1973, facing an energy crisis, the Senate overwhelmingly voted 80–5 for the Trans-Alaska Pipeline Authorization Act.

Dr. Dixy Lee Ray, Chair of the Atomic Energy Commission, issued a December 1973 report recommending a dramatic shift in national energy research priorities. Her report projected that oil imports could drop to zero by 1980. The new program included development of domestic energy sources including coal, oil shale, and nuclear. It also called for accelerated development of petroleum resources in Alaska and on the outer continental shelf.

President Nixon launched Project Independence with a promise that " ... by the end of the decade we will have developed the potential to meet our energy needs without having to rely on any foreign sources."[22] Federal measures instituted to reduce energy usage at the time included setting highway speed limits at 55 mph, establishing year-round daylight savings time throughout the country, and a program to encourage conservation.

During Senate hearings in January 1974, a committee chaired by Senator Henry (Scoop) Jackson (D-Washington), who was considering a presidential run, accused executives of the seven largest oil companies, Exxon, Mobil, Chevron, Amoco, Texaco, Gulf, and Shell, of contriving the energy crisis to reap "unconscionable profits." Oil executives countered that the crisis was the result of " ... a sudden upsurge in demand ... as well as inaction, such as delays in completion of the Alaskan pipeline and in the sale of offshore oil leases." They also saw the chief hope for a long-range energy solution to include alternative sources of energy such as nuclear, coal gasification, and oil shale development.[23] The *New York Times* described the Senate hearings in thermodynamic terms as "a lot of heat and no light."[24]

Following a year of political noise complicated by the Watergate scandal, the Foreign Relations Subcommittee on Multinational Corporations chaired by Senator Frank Church (D-Idaho) concluded, with much less fanfare, that oil companies had behaved responsibly. Not only were oil companies not the cause of the Arab embargo, they "helped blunt the edge of the Arab oil weapon."[25] Of the seven companies accused of making exorbitant profits at the 1974 Senate hearings, only three have survived as independent companies.

After the approval to proceed, TAPS, newly incorporated as the Alyeska Pipeline Services Company, developed a cost estimate based on a much larger 2 million barrel-per-day-capacity system and an upgraded environmental design. The estimate for a 48-inch diameter pipeline system, completed in October 1974, came in at just under $6 billion.[26]

For the next three years, more than 70 thousand people were involved in the building of TAPS at one time or another. Construction was difficult. In return for no strikes, owner companies agreed to lucrative union labor agreements. Initial work included a 28-foot-wide, 400-mile gravel support road (now the Dalton Highway) from Fairbanks to Prudhoe Bay to reduce costly air shipments. It was the first all-season, all-weather highway built across the Arctic Circle in the United States.

More than 500 federal and 800 state permits were needed to comply with strict levels of government oversight and regulations. Approximately 42 thousand welds double-jointed pipe into 80-foot lengths. There were another 66 thousand circumferential welds made in the field.[27]

The final capital cost for TAPS including loan interest was $9.9 billion (nominal), $4 billion more than the original construction estimate. This was a significant overrun but not the tenfold increase always cited. Incredibly, TAPS did cost more to build than the other 220 thousand miles of pipelines in the Lower 48 combined.[28] The transcontinental railroad in 1869 cost less than 10 percent of the final cost for TAPS in real dollars.[29]

Sealift on the Rocks

It remained impractical to construct facilities at Prudhoe Bay due to the extreme conditions. ARCO and BP project management teams in California designed facilities in modular units for fabrication at sites such as the Port of Tacoma, Washington. Barges then moved modules for connection and installation at Prudhoe Bay. It was akin to building a factory as large jigsaw puzzle pieces and assembling them on the North Slope.

Modular design included dynamic modeling to calculate structural allowances for dealing with acceleration stresses at sea. This was critical for barges carrying the heaviest equipment on deck such as turbines and compressors. They could flip and sink. It was also necessary to heat the structures during sealift or they could shatter from cold—like moving giant, ten-story glass buildings.

Just as the Navy Seabees had encountered during their early exploration effort in NPR–A, a small window through the ice of only two weeks was available to tow barges in, offload modules and equipment, and to tow barges out. The first major sealift following the long delay to permit TAPS came during summer 1975.

Tracked crawler-transporters moved preassembled modules with weights ranging from 300 to 1,300 tons from the fabrication sites to barges. The crawlers, some in tandem, were the largest ever used except for those that moved Saturn rockets to launch pads during Apollo moon missions. Pedal to the metal, they could go three-quarters of a mile per hour; normal speed was half that.[30]

After the ocean voyage to Prudhoe Bay, the crawlers moved the modules inland and set them on piling. The piles were sunk 30 to 40 feet into the permafrost and extended eight feet above the surface. Eight feet of air space minimized heat transfer between modules and permanently frozen earth. Otherwise, the heated modules could sink into the permafrost. Modules required positioning to within less than one-inch tolerance at their final locations.[31]

On July 4, a fleet of 47 barges and 22 ocean tugs left Puget Sound, Washington, for the 3,500-mile voyage around Point Barrow to the North Slope. The largest barges were longer and wider than a football field. They were loaded with facilities needed to assure the start of oil production. Total weight was more than 120 thousand tons and total value of cargo for insurance purposes was $1 billion. The fleet itself was worth $250 million. Everything went as planned until a 100-year event.

The flotilla arrived near Wainwright in northwest Alaska in late July. It idled there waiting for the wind to blow ice away from the shore near Point Barrow. But a window through the ice failed to open for the first time in a century. Meteorologists said it was the worst summer weather in northern Alaska since the early 1900s.

In early September, after waiting for weeks, favorable winds finally opened a path and ten barges sneaked around Point Barrow. But, as quickly as it opened, the window slammed shut.

With conditions worsening, a few tugs towed twenty of the barges carrying 27 thousand tons of lighter cargo south to Seward for transport by truck to Prudhoe Bay. Tugs towed two other barges with housing quarters and bridges damaged in gale force winds back to Tacoma, Washington for repair. They would not return until 1976.

The last fifteen barges carrying the most critical equipment for start of oil production continued to idle at Wainwright for one last chance to make a break for the last 180 miles to Prudhoe Bay. If they could not get through, they faced the prospect of wintering somewhere and waiting another year. On September 27, winds moved the ice away from the shoreline and tugs pulled the barges loaded with modules through the eye of a needle.

Two Coast Guard cutters authorized by President Gerald Ford carved a zigzag path through thinner ice on the way to Prudhoe Bay, where they arrived on October 4.[32] There was a rush to off-load the modules as ice packed into the Beaufort Sea, but everything was soon stuck in Prudhoe Bay. Crews drilled through ten feet of ice for ballast water, which immediately froze solid. They would later have to cut the ballast out of the barge holds. Offloading would not resume until January and February after the companies had built an ice and gravel causeway from shore out to the frozen barges.

Sealift weather returned to normal the next summer. ARCO's project management team conducted a study of the Arctic ice-pack to establish a baseline for predicting ice floes in the future. A fleet of 21 barges with 60 thousand tons of cargo worth $200 million headed into Prudhoe Bay in August 1976 as favorable winds blew the ice away from shore as expected. Modules up to 1,300 tons included those for another separation facility and for damaged housing and recreation modules from the previous sealift. The 1976 sealift included all remaining equipment needed to assure production could begin when TAPS was ready.[33]

Moving Modules to Barges

By the end of 1976, TAPS was more than 90 percent complete, but there were mounting problems. The experimental, curious, and stupid had fired a few dozen bullets at the pipeline, requiring replacement of several damaged sections. Quality control audits using radiography found nearly 4 thousand circumferential welds needed repair. The last welds would be made just a month before the start of production.[34]

The effort to get the first North Slope oil to market was coming to an end. Oil imports into the U.S. had increased 60 percent as TAPS was being built. Even so, an economic slowdown predicted for California during 1978 meant there would be a surplus of 500 thousand barrels per day of oil on the West Coast when Alaskan crude finally arrived.

Under the banner of energy independence, foreign export to Asia, in exchange for Middle Eastern oil, was prohibited without an act of Congress and concurrence from the President. Forced to keep Alaskan oil in the country, industry and government scrambled to figure ways to move the oil eastward. At least three proposals with combinations of new and existing pipelines across Canada and the U.S. emerged. They could serve either northern or central states.

Canada, facing its own energy shortage, had phased out exports to the northern states, which made some existing space on Canadian pipelines available. However, none of the pipeline options could be ready in time. Each would increase transportation costs and drive down profits for companies, as well as returns to the state of Alaska. The long ordeal would not end for America's premier petroleum development, even as imports increased and domestic production declined.

Seven years had passed since the Cabinet Task Force had studied the economics of North Slope oil. During 1976, the federal government decided to take a fresh look. The results would contradict the earlier results. Despite popular belief that large reserves meant large profits, updated economic findings questioned the financial viability of the entire Alaskan North Slope endeavor.

FIVE

Winner's Curse

Three Atlantic Refining (later ARCO) geoscientists coined *winner's curse* after studying bids for federal leases in the Gulf of Mexico during the early 1960s. Atlantic won most leases it bid for, but profits from the development projects that followed were not as good as estimated. The scientists decided to find out why. After years of simulating the uncertainty of auctions, they concluded that their company had consistently overbid trying to win every lease.

Although each company at an auction can access the same geophysical data, they had found a systemic bias within Atlantic toward high bids. Too many auction wins had affected profits. Atlantic was winning leases and losing money in the process.

As a result of their study, the scientists proposed a system that restricted bids to approximately 30 percent of the maximum value estimated for each lease. Under the self-imposed limit, the company might bid too high on some leases and too low on others, but would tend to avoid winning everything. A 1971 *Journal of Petroleum Technology* article presented the strategy publicly but few other companies chose to adopt it.[1] The corporate urge to win was just too strong.

In 1969, Amerada Hess and Getty jointly bid for a pair of North Slope leases following the discovery of Prudhoe Bay. They bid over $72 million on one tract just southwest of Prudhoe Bay, which they narrowly won by $160 thousand—a good bid. The companies also bid $18 million on a second tract where the next highest bid was a token one dollar—not so good.[2] In total, Hess and Getty had overspent by over $18 million to win both leases, mostly for the second tract.

Ultimately, it turned out that neither lease provided a commercial discovery and both companies ended up with millions of dollars of losses. The real winner was the state of Alaska, which gladly kept the millions of dollars left on the table. If the companies had been able to use Atlantic's future strategy, they would have lost the first lease, overbid by $5.4 million on the second, and reduced their bottom line losses accordingly. Instead, Hess and Getty became victims of a North Slope version of the winner's curse.

Although winner's curse originally referred to the tendency to overbid at lease auctions, the concept has since been applied to game theory, investments, and signing bonuses for professional athletes. No one ever suspected, however, that the curse could ever extend to the winner of the lease that held Prudhoe Bay, the largest petroleum reservoir in North American history.

Polar Opposite Federal Estimates

Following the 1973 energy crisis, the public demanded that the federal government "do something" about rising oil prices. Congress used the crisis to end legal challenges to Alaskan development and authorized construction of TAPS. The Nixon administration, already trying to manage soaring inflation with wage and price controls, also instituted a complicated program of domestic oil price controls. The Federal Energy Administration (FEA), later incorporated into the Department of Energy during the Carter administration, managed the program. The price controls replaced import controls that had been in place since the Eisenhower administration.

The FEA controlled oil prices under three classifications: (1) domestic "old oil" from wells producing before 1973; (2) domestic "new oil" from wells first producing in 1973 or later; and (3) stripper (from wells producing at ten barrels per day or less) and imported oil at the world market price. In early 1977, per barrel prices for these three tiers were just over $5 at the wellhead, $11 at the wellhead, and between $13 and $14 at the market, respectively.[3]

A complex federal entitlement program tried to balance the costs of buying different tiers of crude oil among domestic refiners. Refiners with access to lower-priced "old oil" paid entitlements to refiners using higher-priced "new oil" or imported crude in order to make the system fair. Different prices for three tiers of oil brought arbitrage opportunities, traders, and some cheaters.

With price controls set to expire in 1981, the federal government wanted to know whether to classify Alaskan North Slope (ANS) crude as "new oil" or imported oil for the first few years of production. In 1976, the FEA contracted with a petroleum consultant to update the economics of ANS development for the first time since 1969. "The Determination of Equitable Pricing Levels for North Slope Alaskan Crude Oil" by Mortada International estimated rates of return under federal price controls in place at the time.[4]

President Nixon's White House Cabinet Task Force (CTF) had predicted exorbitant profits for oil companies on the North Slope. It claimed that Prudhoe Bay oil would be the cheapest in the world. Incredibly, the updated analysis questioned whether Prudhoe Bay might be too expensive to develop even at much higher oil prices. In April 1977, the FEA reported the results of its study to the U.S. Senate barely two months before the start of production.

FEDERAL ESTIMATES FOR PRUDHOE BAY

	CTF $/Barrel(1969)	FEA $/Barrel(1976)
West Coast market price	1.11	13.15
Marine cost	0.30	0.76
TAPS tariff	0.45	4.13
North Slope wellhead price	0.36	8.26
15% IRR	Minimum	Maximum

At the time, Saudi crude delivered to the West Coast of the United States ran between $13 and $14 per barrel or approximately $50 per barrel (2007). The new projected transportation cost—the difference between the average market price at various refineries and the wellhead price on the North Slope—was $4.89 per barrel, substantially higher than in 1969. That left a wellhead price of $8.26 per barrel or $30 per barrel (2007).[5]

The White House Cabinet Task Force had concluded that a Prudhoe Bay development would earn a minimum IRR of 15 percent with wellhead prices as low as 36 cents per barrel.[6] Conversely, the updated FEA study found that even at the highest price permitted under federal law, the IRR would be limited to a maximum of 15 percent.

When a lack of demand on the West Coast later forced one-half of Alaskan oil to the Gulf and East Coasts, marine costs doubled from the FEA estimate. The Cabinet Task Force study had touted North Slope oil as cheap and profitable. Just seven years later, FEA studies figured that ANS was the most expensive in the world and economically challenged.

Melting Rates of Return

The FEA study by Mortada International also modeled an economic case for producing oil from the then speculative Kuparuk River (Kuparuk) and Lisburne formations along with Prudhoe

Bay. Additional production was needed to fill TAPS to its maximum capacity of 2 million barrels per day. The higher throughput would also lower the TAPS tariff (per barrel cost to transport oil through the pipeline). A lower tariff increases wellhead oil price, providing higher revenues for the state of Alaska and the producers. But there was a hitch.

The study found that it cost more to produce additional barrels from the new reservoirs rather than from Prudhoe Bay alone. The higher incremental cost per barrel offset any benefits from a lower pipeline tariff. As a result, the calculated rate of return fell from just under 15 percent for producing Prudhoe Bay alone to just over 14 percent for producing more expensive Kuparuk and Lisburne too.[7] In other words, producing more oil after supergiant Prudhoe Bay increased gross revenue but reduced profit margins because of higher costs.

An exploration venture in a virgin area such as the North Slope is always risky. There was agreement among the federal government, the state of Alaska, and the oil companies that the rate of return for successful fields needed to be high enough to cover the losses on future drilling to encourage more Arctic exploration. However, questions remained about the actual level of risk involved.

The Mortada study used a risk factor to adjust calculated rates of return for future well failures. Mortada estimated that one in seven future exploration wells might result in another commercial discovery. The associated risk factor when applied to the economic calculation lowered the expected rate of return for total ANS production from 14 to 12 percent.

ARCO, BP, and Exxon testified to Congress that they generally agreed with Mortada's methodology except for the exploration risk factor. On average, only one in nine wildcat (speculative) exploration wells found commercial oil worldwide. The companies suggested a more realistic exploration success rate of one commercial discovery for every ten exploration wells on the North Slope.[8]

In hindsight, the oil companies were also too optimistic about exploration potential on the North Slope. Exploration drilling for the period from 1964 through 2004 resulted in 53 discoveries from 386 tries. Although one in seven wells found hydrocarbons, only half of those met the technical and economic criteria to allow commercial production.[9] In other words, there has been one commercial discovery for every fifteen exploration wells—less than a 7 percent historical success rate—on the North Slope.

A risk factor based on actual exploration success retroactively applied to the FEA study methodology further reduces the predicted rate of return from 12 to 10 percent. Before oil companies had produced the first North Slope barrel, the projected rate of return was insufficient to support further exploration and development. The expected rate of return would not cover the cost of capital. Nor would returns provide an incentive for companies to drill more exploration wells.

The 1970s were the years of the economic misery index as inflation and interest rates soared. Inflation in 1977 was 6 percent and grew to 13 percent by 1980. Prime interest rates would reach 20 percent by 1980 as well.[10] Borrowing billions of dollars at inflated interest rates to finance a risky, grassroots venture that at best might earn a 10 to 12 percent rate of return was an economic nonstarter.

The investment banking firm of Morgan Stanley & Company, Inc., testified to Congress that oil companies should not have undertaken ANS development in the first place. Morgan Stanley told the U.S. Senate that a projected rate of return at 12 percent

MELTING RATES OF RETURN

FEA Study Case	IRR (%)
Prudhoe Bay only	15
Prudhoe Bay, Kuparuk, Lisburne	14
Prudhoe Bay, Kuparuk, Lisburne, 1 in 7	12
Prudhoe Bay, Kuparuk, Lisburne, 1 in 15*	10

*Actual exploration success

would have precluded financing. Furthermore, they could not accept such a low rate of return as adequate for a project of such high risk.

North Sea developments with high costs and heavy government take averaged rates of return of 22 percent at the time. According to Morgan Stanley, a 12 percent rate of return might be appropriate for a regulated industry but not for a high-risk petroleum development on the North Slope. Economic consultants for the Alaska Federation of Natives testified that the minimum rate of return acceptable for an exploration venture in the Arctic should be 40 to 50 percent. Most consulting firms recommended a range of 20 to 25 percent. That rate of return would cover the cost of capital, the risk of future failure, and the cost of transporting oil thousands of miles to markets.[11]

In a February 1977 *Fortune* magazine article, "My Case for National Planning," Thornton Bradshaw, president of ARCO, made a shocking proposal. He wanted the federal government to lead the nation to energy security through centralized planning. He contended that the U.S. economy was no longer a total free-enterprise system. Bradshaw suggested that federal oil price controls should be eliminated except for the price of domestic crude.[12]

Bradshaw wanted the federal government to permanently manage domestic prices as an incentive for industry to meet national production goals. Although the proposal from an oil executive was surprising to many, it is more understandable in the context of the results of the FEA economic study. ARCO had staked its vision on becoming *the* domestic oil company focused solely on Alaska. That vision was melting away along with the expected rate of return.

The FEA skirted the sensitive issue of marginal economics in its April 15, 1977, report to Congress, commenting, "It is apparent ... that any effort to determine the appropriate level of prices for ANS oil that will provide a fair return on existing investments and provide incentives for further development is fraught with uncertainty and speculation."[13] In other words, the FEA and the U.S. Senate knew from the start that North Slope producers would not achieve a satisfactory rate of return under federal oil price controls.

There had been a decade of hype about ANS development in the media. Expectations by oil company shareholders, the federal government, and the state of Alaska were high. There had been costly court fights over TAPS permits and billions of dollars in early investment. There were also associated national security and energy independence implications. ARCO, BP, and Exxon could only hope for even higher oil prices, lower taxes, and reduced development costs.

A *New York Times* story reported that high transportation costs would limit profits from North Slope oil. The article inferred that cost overruns for TAPS were the major reason for the marginal economics. In fact, the real problems cited in the FEA study were that oil prices were too low, development costs too high, and taxes too heavy. Moreover, the *Times* article contended that the large oil price increases following the energy crisis in 1973 were the only thing that could keep Alaskan oil from becoming "industry's most burdensome white elephant."[14]

Coincident with the FEA study results, a report by the Central Intelligence Agency (CIA) warned that world oil production had peaked. Demand would soon exceed supply and oil prices would rise forever.[15] Despite the mixed federal messages, the highest oil prices allowed were not high enough to support North Slope development and, even without federal controls, never would be. In fact, despite occasional price spikes and political threats of windfall profits taxes, oil prices trended lower until the new millennium.

A Brief Sigh of Relief

Friday, June 17, 1977, was clear and mild on the shores of the Beaufort Sea at Prudhoe Bay. It was one of those days when the farthest peaks of the Brooks Range, more than 120 miles to the south, were visible all the way across what Alaskans call "the Slope." It is a treeless plain that slopes gently from the northern foothills of the Brooks Range to the Arctic Ocean—an area larger than Idaho.

A spongy cover of peat on the three-foot layer of tundra had turned a dark shade of golden green. Some relatively warm weather just above freezing had tried to melt the last remnants of snow and ice on the Arctic desert as summer approached. Directly below this surface activity sat 2 thousand feet of permafrost, an impermeable layer of frozen earth.

Forces of nature had trapped surface water molecules in a continuous seasonal process since Alaska and the rest of North America drifted close to their current locations a hundred million years ago, give or take. The Slope's surface would soon turn into swamp muck as residual moisture from barely five inches of annual precipitation failed to penetrate permafrost. Ironically, Arctic cold makes the North Slope a swampy desert every summer.[16]

Mosquitoes in the millions, maybe the billions, swarmed around small, shallow ponds that provided temporary moisture for the tundra cover. Summer solstice was just a couple of days away. The longest day of the year is hard to tell apart from any other day at Prudhoe Bay from early May to early August. There are no sunsets.

At five o'clock on this June evening, ARCO's control room at one of its recently completed separation facilities finally received *the* phone call. Alyeska Pipeline Service Company's operators at the northernmost pump station on the brand-new 800-mile Trans-Alaska Pipeline System announced, "We're ready for you to start sending us some oil up to Skid 50." Skid 50, located just upstream of TAPS, is the name for the point separating oil production on the North Slope from pipeline transportation south to the Valdez Marine Terminal. Two large pipelines carrying crude from each half of the Prudhoe Bay field converge there.

At startup, ARCO and BP had installed three of six planned separation facilities costing hundreds of millions of dollars each. Several gravel-padded, multiple-welled drill sites were scattered

around the field near the best reservoir targets. Wells directionally drilled from the pads penetrated through permafrost into reservoir targets thousands of feet under the tundra. There were no
surface (sucker rod) pumps on the North Slope because there
was enough reservoir pressure for flow to reach the surface on
its own.

At 6 P.M., production personnel informed the Alyeska pipeline crew that they were ready. Three football fields in distance
from the control room, in an interconnected module containing crude-oil pumps, an operator turned a 10-inch valve on one
of the shipping pumps. Just as the first barrel of North Slope oil
should have flowed, nothing happened.

After nearly two decades of blood, sweat and tears, waiting
a few more minutes for the first North Slope barrel did not really
seem to matter that much anymore. At 9:29 P.M., the ARCO operator tried again and turned a big red wheel on the actuator to
open the 10-inch valve on a parallel pump. Oil soon moved
through flow meters into the 34-inch-diameter gathering pipeline, connecting the separation facility with TAPS. Later, the stub-
born parallel pump finally decided to participate as well. BP also
started sending oil from their half of the field.

At midnight Saturday, June 18, the sun shone high in the
Arctic sky and a caribou enjoyed a late-night snack beside the
gravel road between the separation facility and the Prudhoe Bay
Operations Center. While most Americans slept, oil production
had just begun from the largest petroleum development in North
American history. The next step involved moving oil into the
pipeline system.

It turned cold and rainy on the North Slope on Sunday,
June 19, when shortly after midnight operators at the separation
facility received another message: "Pump Station advised they
are ready to start flow to tanks. ... So, gentlemen, start your
engines." As large, 34-inch gate valves opened, Prudhoe Bay oil
began to flow away from the North Slope into TAPS storage tanks
for the first time at 12:15 A.M. The oil level built in the tanks on

Sunday as media and dignitaries arrived in Anchorage for a press conference.[17]

The Department of the Interior had authorized flow into the pipeline beginning 9 A.M. on Monday, June 20, 1977. After the press conference, the entourage flew the 650 miles to the North Slope to witness and report on the movement of the first barrel south to Valdez and the Lower 48. On a near freezing first day of Arctic summer, Alyeska launched a half-ton plastic cylindrical plug—called a *pig*—loaded with instrumentation into the 48-inch pipeline, followed by hot crude oil. Pigs flow along with the oil and clean accumulated wax, check for corrosion, and detect deformation.

There were no wireless internet connections, portable computers, cell phones, or e-mails in 1977. Pocket calculators were in the process of hammering a final stake into the heart of the slide rule. Keuffel & Esser Co., which had once sold 20 thousand "slip-sticks" per month during the 1950s, had donated its engraving equipment to the Smithsonian Institution in Washington, D.C.[18]

Instead, a high-tech teletype message circulated around ARCO project management offices announcing the event:

> The oil entered the pipeline at 10:06 AM Alaska time. The pig departed according to plan, attended by line walkers and the press. The producers are producing 100,000 barrels a day through Flow Station 1, Flow Station 2, and G.C. 1 [separation facilities], and expect to increase that rate to 300,000 barrels a day over the next thirty-six hours.[19]

As the pig scraped and cleaned the pipeline, reporters and technicians followed alongside listening for squeals. They touched each section of the pipeline to feel for warmth as oil progressed toward Valdez for the first time. The pig, the hot oil, and the cluster of people moved at the breakneck speed of around one mile per hour. Pipeline insulation kept the oil above its wax point so TAPS would not become the world's longest Chapstick. After the ceremonial start, the press and dignitaries left, but the first barrel of oil was still a month and a half from a refinery and a market in the Lower 48.

Technicians maintained constant surveillance on the first, slow, careful trip all the way to the huge storage tanks at the Valdez Marine Terminal. During the following 38½ days, oil traveled across mountain ranges, over or under hundreds of rivers and streams, and through the most seismically active areas in the United States. More than half the pipeline zigzags above ground on supports designed to allow it to expand and contract with temperature changes and to adjust to ground movement during earthquakes.

Despite intense training and precautions, three human errors by operators caused pipeline stoppages before the first oil made it to Valdez. The most serious of the three incidents took place on July 8 about forty miles south of Fairbanks. A worker, not following procedures practiced for weeks, opened a valve blocking oil from a filter undergoing maintenance at a pump station. Oil spewed through the exposed filter onto the combustion section of a nearby turbine that was driving a pipeline pump. The result was an explosion, a fatality, several injuries, and millions of dollars in damage. The mishap shut the whole process down for days.[20]

There was also an incident of external vandalism when some young entrepreneurs placed three dynamite charges against the pipeline to see what would happen. Fortunately, the experiment did not result in a shutdown although the blasts damaged some pipeline insulation.[21] It took a month to fill TAPS with over 9 million barrels of oil.

The ocean tanker fleet for the three major and five minor pipeline owners had been queuing in Prince William Sound at Valdez, awaiting the oil's arrival. On August 1, the *S.S. ARCO*

Juneau departed a loading berth at Valdez with the first shipment of 900 thousand barrels for delivery to the Cherry Point
Refinery on the shores of Washington's Puget Sound. Subsequent
tankers began moving oil to California; others traveled to the
Gulf Coast through the Panama Canal. On September 17, an
ocean tanker delivered Prudhoe Bay crude for the first time to
the East Coast to a refinery in Delaware.

As the first barrels of Prudhoe Bay reserves worked their way
into the market, another delivery took place in the Lower 48. The
Strategic Petroleum Reserve, a special storage facility in a subsurface salt dome in Louisiana, also received its first shipment
of crude oil. Dependence on foreign oil had become an even
greater concern during and after the Yom Kippur War in 1973.
The concern spurred both the authorization of TAPS and a strategic reserve that could offset temporary supply disruptions
during similar crises in the future.[22]

Before Prudhoe Bay production, the U.S. was importing 42
percent of its oil, which amounted to over 7.3 million barrels

A Separation Facility on the North Slope (1977)

per day. Incredibly, as Arctic oil flowed to the Lower 48 and federal oil flowed into the Strategic Petroleum Reserve, a Gallup poll found that 52 percent of Americans were unaware that the nation needed to import any oil to handle its energy needs. It also found that 33 percent of the public thought the country was energy independent and 15 percent did not know either way. Most polled were also unaware that record oil imports caused record trade deficits.[23]

The Ordeal Continues

In mid-1977, when Alaskan crude was finally heading to market, an economic slowdown had caused an oil glut on the West Coast. This forced one-half of the incoming crude to find domestic markets farther away through the Panama Canal. The canal could not handle the largest crude oil carriers, which made it necessary to transfer crude to smaller vessels. All of this meant higher transportation costs and more environmental risk.

The producers and the state of Alaska requested permission from the federal government to swap ANS for higher-quality Saudi crude on the world market. Saudi crude could go to the East Coast while ANS could go to Asia in exchange. This would lower shipping costs, increase profits, raise returns for the state of Alaska, and reduce refining costs.

Congress had banned foreign export of Alaskan oil in the name of "energy independence" when it authorized construction of TAPS. The export ban forced companies to make extensive modifications to domestic refineries in order to handle ANS crude. Longer shipping distances through the Panama Canal pushed returns for producers as well as the state of Alaska even lower.

The maritime industry and its labor unions also lobbied Congress to ban exports of Alaskan crude oil. In addition, they wanted to prevent the use of lower-cost foreign tankers and crews. The Merchant Marine Act of 1920 (Jones Act) requires that

Historical Tanker Routes

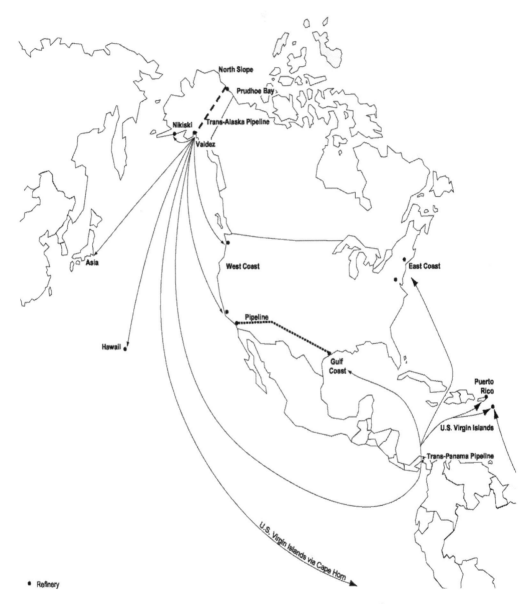

Source: GAO/RCED-99-191 Alaskan North Slope Oil.

ships carrying cargo between U.S. ports must be U.S.-built, flagged, owned, and crewed.[24]

Congress supported the maritime unions in order to stimulate the domestic shipping industry. Because of the export ban, American shipyards built more than fifty tankers to move ANS crude. That was half of all domestic-flagged tankers completed during the 1970s and 1980s.[25] In 2010, there were just fifteen ocean tankers left in ANS service.

As of summer 2009, more than 20 thousand ocean tanker trips had carried Arctic oil from Valdez to mainly domestic refineries. An average tanker carried about 800 thousand barrels.[26] Unfortunately, the most famous one is the *Exxon Valdez* that ran aground in Prince William Sound on Good Friday 1989. The tanker leaked 250 thousand barrels, or about one-fifth of its cargo. As a direct result of the spill, the Oil Pollution Act of 1990 required that all North Slope crude tankers have double hulls by 2015.[27]

According to the chief economist for the U.S. Senate Interior Committee at the time, Congress enacted the export ban largely out of spite to make ANS less profitable.[28] Two decades later, a tanker exported the first ANS oil. It left Valdez for Asia on May 31, 1996, six months after Congress finally allowed Alaska to join the world market.[29]

Shipping Costs for ANS in 1996

Destination	Tanker Days	L48 Pipeline $/Barrel	Total $/Barrel
Asia	30	—	2.64
Gulf Coast	41	0.82	7.15
Virgin Islands	84	—	2.35
Mid-Continent	16	2.17	3.80
West Coast	5–18	—	1.63

Source: GAO/RCED-99-191 Alaskan North Slope Oil.

Exports were short-lived and less than 100 million barrels in total. There have been no exports since 2004.[30] A 1999 General Accounting Office (GAO) report determined that the federal ban on exporting Alaskan oil in the name of "energy independence" had increased tanker costs by up to $1.30 per barrel on average.[31] In 2009, annual tanker trips from Valdez averaged just more than 300, about one-third the 1989 peak, as North Slope production continued to decline.[32]

Rules established by the Interstate Commerce Commission (ICC) determined the regulated pipeline tariff. Regulations allowed pipeline owners a maximum 7 percent rate of return on their investment. Based on the guidelines, TAPS owners filed tariffs with the ICC ranging from $6.04 to $6.44 per barrel. However, before a drop of oil entered TAPS, lawyers for the state of Alaska and the Justice Department were already in court disputing the calculation.[33]

A former Watergate prosecutor hired by the state of Alaska claimed that construction mismanagement and alleged indifference to cost caused $1.5 billion in overruns. The state argued that the owners, essentially ARCO, BP, and Exxon, did not care how much the pipeline cost. They could recover any overruns through a higher tariff. The state wanted the cost overruns subtracted from the tariff calculation. The ICC initially agreed. It set interim rates 20 percent lower than filed tariffs even though the first barrels were halfway to Valdez.[34]

Attorneys for the TAPS owners argued that interim rates established by the ICC did not follow past federal procedure. Interim rates reduced the rate of return on the pipeline investment. An interesting twist is that a lower tariff decreases profits for pipeline owners but increases profits for oil producers. The largest pipeline owners, also the major producers, found themselves on both sides of the issue.

Attorneys kept busy and made a lot of money before the parties reached an agreement in 1985. Total legal fees had reached

$150 million. The Federal Energy Regulatory Commission (FERC), then responsible for pipeline regulation, approved a tariff settlement agreement between the pipeline owners and the state of Alaska. The maximum tariff allowed pipeline owners a 6.4 percent real rate of return on their investment from the settlement forward.[35]

The first barrels were arriving at West Coast refineries before the FEA decided to classify ANS crude as imported oil.[36] Even at the highest price allowed under federal price controls, high transportation costs from Alaska reduced wellhead oil price on the North Slope to below that for "new oil" in the Lower 48. The bonanza of oil profits originally predicted by federal government economists and experts did not exist and never would.

With little other economic activity in the state of Alaska, there was only one deep pocket for government to hit up for revenue to fund spending—oil companies and their shareholders. According to Alaska's then petroleum revenue director, "There is not enough economic activity to support this state if all you do here is shoot game, catch fish, and cut down trees … there is no one else but the oil industry to hit for revenues. It's the only deep pocket in town."[37] ARCO, BP, and Exxon had won an Arctic prize. Developing it would prove to be a supergiant version of the winner's curse.

The startup of Prudhoe Bay and TAPS was an engineering and construction marvel. The American Society of Civil Engineers named TAPS the outstanding engineering achievement of 1978.[38] A less sanguine *Oil and Gas Journal* editorial summed up the prevailing mood among those involved: "Completion of a pipeline which adds 1.2 million barrels per day to oil supply ought to be cause for celebration. Instead there is a sigh of relief that the ordeal is over."[39]

However, the economic ordeal—the profit-sharing trilemma—had only just begun.

SIX

Shrinking Prize

During summer 1979, as production from Alaska ramped up, President Jimmy Carter delivered a nationally televised "Crisis of Confidence" speech declaring the moral equivalent of war on energy use in America. He told the nation that energy prices were "going through the roof" and that the world was running out of oil. He was replacing President Nixon's Project Independence with a new energy plan. President Carter guaranteed that with his plan the "nation will never use more foreign oil than we did in 1977—never."[1] Alaskan oil seemed to be coming to the market at the perfect time.

Despite presidential warnings of an impending worldwide shortage, supply easily covered demand during the 1980s and 1990s. New sources appeared from the North Sea and Mexico, as well as Alaska, while Saudi Arabia flooded the world to maintain its market share. Coupled with less demand in the U.S., the world supply glut forced oil prices lower over the next two decades. And imports into the country continued to increase as domestic supplies decreased. Lower prices affected investment

Domestic Oil Price ($/Barrel)

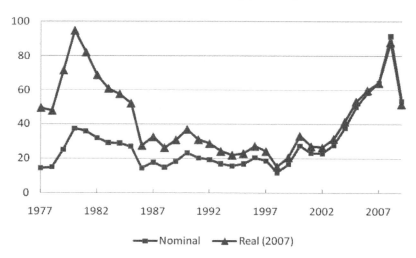

Data Source: Energy Information Agency (EIA).

returns for oil developments, especially in high-cost areas such as Alaska.

Field operators initially planned to recover 9.6 billion barrels from Prudhoe Bay. The FEA study by Mortada International had projected that companies might recover a combined 11.3 billion barrels from Prudhoe Bay, Kuparuk, and Lisburne, should the latter two fields eventually pan out. Continuous improvement of reservoir management techniques along with a host of enhanced oil recovery (EOR) projects have since boosted ultimate recovery from Prudhoe Bay to 13.7 billion barrels.

Operators plan to recover approximately 60 percent of the original oil in place from the Prudhoe Bay reservoir. Similar EOR efforts have also increased recovery from Kuparuk since it began producing in 1982, although not as dramatically. Lisburne is a less porous and permeable limestone/dolomite reservoir that has proven disappointing as a producer.

Tectonic processes that formed elephants on the North Slope also deposited several smaller accumulations at various depths

ANS Oil Reserves through 2009 (Billion Barrels)

Field	Produced	Ultimate
Prudhoe Bay	11.7	13.7
Kuparuk	2.2	2.8
Smaller Reservoirs	2.3	4.8
Total	16.2	21.3

Data Source: Alaska Department of Natural Resources.

near the Arctic coast. Companies discovered many of them while exploring and drilling for the larger fields. In 2010, approximately two dozen reservoirs are producing oil; nevertheless, Prudhoe Bay and Kuparuk, both discovered in the late 1960s, have supplied seven-eighths of all production.[2] Prudhoe Bay alone is responsible for approximately three-fourths of the total.

A few of the smaller fields on the North Slope are remote from central infrastructure and have individual processing facilities.

ANS Oil Production

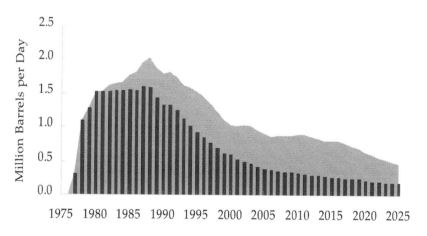

Total ANS ■ Prudhoe Bay

Data Source: Alaska Department of Natural Resources.

U.S. Oil Production (Billion Barrels)

	Period		
	1859–2009	*1959–2009*	*1977–2009*
Texas	63.8	41.9	21.9
Louisiana	27.7	23.0	11.0
California	28.0	16.5	10.6
Oklahoma	15.0	7.1	3.5
Alaska	16.9	16.9	16.2
U.S.	199.6	139.3	84.5

Source: Energy Information Agency (EIA).

Most are satellites of larger fields, not commercial on their own, which share spare capacity to reduce production costs. Smaller fields will supply most North Slope oil in the future, as the elephants fade away.

It took just thirty years to drain seven-eighths of the proven oil reserves on the North Slope, including nearly seven-eighths of Prudhoe Bay. In terms of total U.S. production, despite having the two largest-producing oilfields in the country for most of the period since 1977, Alaska still ranks behind Texas. At current forecasts, that will not change.

More Oil, Less Revenue

ANS is one of over 160 crudes traded on worldwide markets.[3] It is a little denser and contains slightly more sulfur than West Texas Intermediate (WTI), the benchmark used to value crude types in the U.S. since the late 1980s. Brent is the benchmark most widely used outside the United States. From 1977 through 1981, under federal price controls, the cost of imported oil determined the ANS market price. After price decontrol, the average cost of oil delivered to refineries set the market price from 1981 to 1988.

Since the late 1980s, crude that is higher in quality than a benchmark sells at a premium to it while lower quality varieties sell at a discount. ANS is intermediate quality crude that costs more to refine into petroleum products such as gasoline, jet fuel, and diesel than crudes closer in quality to WTI. The quality price differential between WTI and the ANS averaged $2.32 per barrel from 1988 through 2005.[4] That resulted in a market discount of $22 billion (nominal) or $32 billion (2007).

The difference between ANS market and wellhead prices is the cost of transportation from the North Slope to various refineries. Alternatively, the cost of transportation reduces the market price when "netted back" from refineries to the wellhead, the point of production on the North Slope. The so-called *netback* or wellhead price determines the value of production taxable by state and federal governments, and ultimately, the net profit left for producers and shareholders to share.

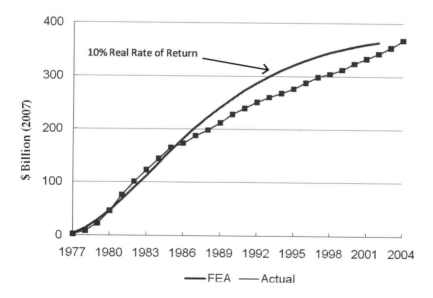

Cumulative ANS Wellhead Revenue

Wellhead revenue is production multiplied by wellhead price. The FEA study projected that 11.3 billion barrels of production would yield $100 billion (1976) or $364 billion (2007) in cumulative wellhead revenue over 25 years, assuming a flat oil price adjusted for inflation. When two decades of lower oil prices followed, it took two more years and 2.5 billion additional barrels, nearly all the reserves in giant Kuparuk, to reach the FEA projection.

Since ANS is thousands of miles from refineries and markets, transportation costs are very high. Within Alaska, these include tariffs for pipelines on the North Slope as well as the TAPS tariff. Outside Alaska, transportation costs include shipping on ocean tankers and tariffs for Lower 48 pipelines.

It cost an average $6.95 per barrel (nominal) to move 15.1 billion barrels of ANS totaling $105 billion (nominal) or $207 billion (2007). Together, crude quality and transportation costs shrunk the value of 15.1 billion barrels of ANS production by approximately 40 percent at the wellhead.

Complex facilities produce and process petroleum on the North Slope. From 1968 through 2003, more than 330 barges delivered 1.3 million tons of material and modules stuffed with processing equipment around Point Barrow through the annual summer windows through the ice.[5] According to a General Accounting Office study that examined the future cost of removing North Slope infrastructure, there were 13 production facilities, 14 industrial plants, 5 docks and causeways, and 5 airstrips as of January 2000.[6] Power generation, gas compression, and water injection require over 3 million horsepower supplied by natural gas turbines and electric motors. Installed horsepower is equivalent to fifty 747 airliners flying at cruising speed around the clock.

The Prudhoe Bay reservoir is porous and permeable sandstone found 9 thousand feet below the earth's surface. It contains layers of water, oil, and natural gas. Water is heaviest and natural gas is lightest. Wells penetrate two thousand feet of permafrost from drill sites/well pads and then angle or kick off, some horizontally, to reservoir targets that can be miles away. Large-diameter flow lines take fizzy well fluid from well pads to separation facilities situated across the field.

Crude oil must be free of natural gas, water, and impurities before TAPS can transport it to Valdez and on to ocean tankers. Several large, horizontal vessels at each separation facility gradually lower the pressure of well fluid in three or four stages to atmospheric pressure. The fizzy mixture ends up as individual streams of oil, natural gas, and produced water.

Pumps at each separation facility return produced water to the reservoir for pressure maintenance. Seawater treatment and injection plants process and pressurize water from the Beaufort Sea into the oil column in a secondary recovery process called *waterflooding*. Centralized facilities take natural gas produced with oil for further processing, compression, and reinjection into the reservoir to produce more oil and to conserve natural gas.

Finally, crude free of natural gas and water heads to Pump Station 1, where it mixes with oil from other oilfields as well as natural gas liquids (NGL). NGL includes propane, butane, and natural gasoline condensed by chilling natural gas. Lean gas remains after recovering NGL and is reinjected into the reservoir. After processing and metering, all liquid petroleum goes to TAPS.

Transportation of oil across Alaska is a roller-coaster ride like no other. TAPS crosses three mountain ranges and dozens of major rivers. It encounters immense elevation changes, peaking at Atigun Pass in the Brooks Range at more than 4,700 feet. Large storage tanks at the Valdez Marine Terminal can hold the entire 9 million barrel capacity of the pipeline.

Several ramps cross over the pipeline to accommodate caribou migration. In hindsight, it was learned the caribou prefer navigating under the pipeline and often use it as a snow shield. A few signs surreptitiously placed at ramps in the early days of TAPS implored caribou to use them since they were expensive.

Alaska North Slope Schematic

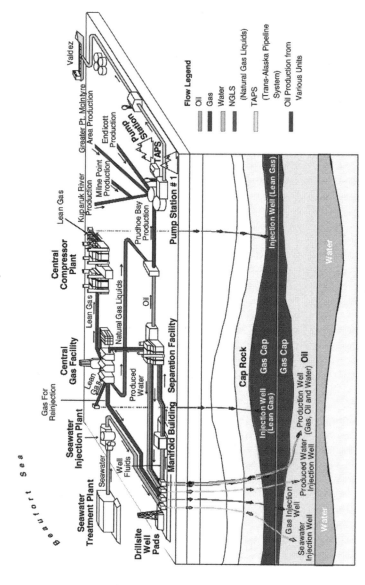

Source: GAO-02-357 Alaska's North Slope Oil.

TAPS Profile

Elevation (Feet): 0, 1000, 2000, 3000, 4000, 5000

Pipeline Milepost: 0, 50, 100, 150, 200, 250, 300, 350, 400, 450, 500, 550, 600, 650, 700, 750, 800

Labels: PS-1, PS-2, PS-3, PS-4, PS-5, PS-6, PS-7, PS-8, PS-9, PS-10, PS-12

ATIGUN PASS, ISABEL PASS, THOMPSON PASS, Valdez

Hydraulic Gradient

Source: "APSC Strategic Reconfiguration," http://www.alyeska-pipe.com/sr.html.

101

ALASKA'S SHRINKING BARREL (15.1 BILLION BARRELS THROUGH 2005)

	$/Barrel		$ Billion	
	Nominal	2007	Nominal	2007
ANS Market Value	22.61	39.23	342	593
Transportation Costs outside Alaska to Markets	(2.78)	(6.03)	(42)	(91)
TAPS Transportation Costs	(4.17)	(7.68)	(63)	(116)
Wellhead Revenue	15.66	25.52	237	386
TAPS Revenue	4.17	7.68	63	116
Total Revenue	19.83	33.20	300	502
Capital and Operating Costs	(6.89)	(13.97)	(104)	(211)
Net Cash available to Share	12.94	19.23	196	291

TAPS is both a cost and a revenue generator, earning a regulated profit. State and federal governments tax both production (wellhead) and pipeline (TAPS) revenue within Alaska (shaded). The net cash available for sharing remains after deducting capital and operating costs for both ANS production and TAPS. Fair sharing of the net cash among the state of Alaska, the federal government, and oil companies presents a profits trilemma. A cash flow table and data sources are included in the Appendix.

The original TAPS design included twelve pump stations (PS), although the companies built just eleven. PS-5 acted as a pressure relief station at the bottom of Atigun Pass under the weight of thousands of feet of heavy oil flowing over the Brooks Range. By 1997, TAPS needed only six pump stations to handle declining oil production. In 2010, TAPS used just four.[7] By then, it took nearly two weeks at 2½ miles per hour for a barrel to travel the 800-mile trip from the North Slope, about three times what it took at peak throughput.[8]

Capital expenditure (Capex), including finding costs, for the complicated system of exploration, wells, and facilities on the North Slope totaled $46.8 billion (nominal) or $98.1 billion (2007), while Capex for TAPS added another $9.9 billion (nominal) or $37.2 billion (2007). ANS operating expenditure (Opex) averaged approximately $2 per barrel (nominal) for 15.1 billion barrels, while TAPS Opex averaged approximately $1 per barrel (nominal). Total expenditure for both the North Slope and TAPS came to $104.1 billion (nominal) or $211.3 billion (2007), nearly identical to total transportation cost. The pre-tax net cash left to divvy up among the three stakeholders after deducting costs was $196 billion (nominal) or $291 billion (2007). The state of Alaska took its share of the net pie first.

Heavy Taxes

Oil companies and their shareholders hoped to earn a profit from their ANS investment after paying taxes to all forms of government on both production and pipeline revenue. Throughout history, people have mined minerals for use as money. Rulers and nations historically owned the underground rights to minerals and a royalty became the sovereign's share of any discovery.[9]

In the early days of the oil age, private leases in America adopted the Anglo-Saxon rule of a one-eighth or 12½ percent royalty. This percentage assumed that an operator would earn a profit of 25 percent and split it equally with the landowner.[10] The state of Alaska, as sovereign and landowner, collects the traditional royalty of 12½ percent of gross wellhead value for petroleum produced from most ANS leases.

In addition to royalty, the state of Alaska assesses a production or severance tax on gross wellhead value, which is a one-time tax on the extraction of a nonrenewable resource. Lease agreements determine the terms for royalty and are constant. Production tax, on the other hand, has become the "fair share" tax that the state has regularly increased to extract more money to finance its spending.

The state raised its production tax over twelvefold during the period between its Constitutional Convention in 1955 and before the first barrel of oil entered TAPS in 1977. For the period 1977 through 2005, production tax averaged just over 10 percent of the gross wellhead value. The state of Alaska took nearly one-fourth of gross wellhead value from a combination of royalty and production tax before assessing other taxes.

In 1972, during the delay in getting a permit to build TAPS, Governor William Egan (D) proposed a property tax. Egan wanted an annual tax of 2 percent on the assessed value of future North Slope and TAPS infrastructure to accrue to the state. Local governments along the pipeline corridor led by Fairbanks successfully fought in court to get a share of the proposed tax that passed during the 1973 legislative session. Since then, state and municipalities along the TAPS route have shared property tax.[11]

In 1974, as TAPS construction began, Jay Hammond (R) defeated William Egan (D) for governor. During the campaign, Hammond claimed that Egan's spending had caused a budget gap and proposed a new way to close it. In Alaska, regardless of political party, that means finding a new way to tax oil companies. The Hammond administration hired a consulting firm to devise a unique corporate income tax.

The result was a "unitary" income tax that included adjustments for income outside the state's borders. The state of Alaska benefits from an oil company's income produced elsewhere. For oil companies, the tax is 9.4 percent of the portion of world-wide federal taxable income apportioned to Alaska based on property, pipeline, and production revenues. Alaska selectively requires oil companies to add back any foreign income taxes deducted in determining their federal taxable income. Oil companies must report foreign income as well.[12]

In 1976, the state of Alaska was running a $300 million deficit on a $600 million budget with ANS production still a year away. The legislature decided to tax oil reserves in the ground as a prepayment on future production. In effect, the state gave itself an interest-free loan paid by oil companies as a reserves tax to avoid going broke.[13] Over the years, there have also been a few legal settlements that have grabbed headlines, but they are small in relation to total state take. The biggest was in the early 1990s, when the three major producers agreed to pay a total of $736 million in additional back charges for disputed royalty payments.

Alaska's share or take from 15.1 billion barrels of ANS production came to 41 percent of the $291 million (2007) net. Royalty and production tax made up more than three-fourths

ALASKA'S SHARE OF 15.1 BILLION BARRELS

Revenue Source	$Billion (nominal)	$Billion (2007)
Royalty	29.6	48.2
Production Tax	24.1	40.6
Property Tax	6.9	11.3
Income Tax	7.0	12.5
Leases	1.0	2.1
Legal	0.9	2.0
Reserves Tax	0.5	1.9
Total	70.0	118.6

Data Source: Alaska Department of Revenue, Tax Division.

of the total. After Alaska collects its wedge, the federal government takes its slice via a corporate income tax.

Federal corporate tax derived from actual state collections comes to $27 billion (nominal) or $50 billion (2007). The federal government also collected approximately $5 billion (nominal) or $12 billion (2007) in Windfall Profits Tax (WPT) from North Slope oil producers. The federal government instituted the WPT after removing oil price controls in 1979. WPT was much less than expected since oil prices were generally below the federal reference price while the excise tax was in place. Total federal take came to $32 billion (nominal) or $62 billion (2007), 21 percent of the net pie.

The effective federal tax rate of 21 percent was approximately one-half the average federal corporate income tax rate over the investment period. Lower federal returns were not the result of any loophole as often charged. Instead, high costs and increasing state taxes reduced the federal share when deducted from federal corporate income tax returns.

Combined federal and state government take was 62 percent of the $291 billion (2007) net. Producers shared the remaining 38 percent based on their individual ownership percentages in the various oilfields. In return, they provided the financing and took all the operational risk.

Investment Life

In *The Age of Oil* (Praeger 2006), the author, an executive with a national oil company, contends, " … high [oil] prices of the 1970s made very profitable various high-profile investments in areas and fields whose development would have been otherwise delayed by their higher costs and greater technical difficulty. This was the case with Alaska."[14] In fact, even as oil prices doubled after the Iranian revolution, Alaska was far from becoming very profitable.

By the end of 1978, ARCO, BP, and Exxon had shipped 500 million barrels out of Alaska, and Prudhoe Bay was producing 1.2 million barrels per day. In February 1979, a *Business Week* magazine article reported that soaring costs, state taxes, and environmental disputes had forced most of the industry away from Alaska. Annualized profit from Prudhoe Bay was barely 9 percent, less than companies were earning in the North Sea.

Twenty oil companies had already packed up and left the North Slope. U.S. Senator Ted Stevens (R-Alaska) warned, "If that continues, and the Alaskan people get the feeling that Prudhoe Bay is the first and last major field, I think the attitude of the legislature and the executive branch will change radically. The [remaining] oil companies will face a potential for increased taxation and state participation in their activities."[15]

There had been more than a dozen changes to state taxes on oil companies during the 1970s. Standard Oil of Ohio (later BP) Chairman Alton T. Whitehouse complained, "The Alaskans are raising moneys unrelated to their fiscal needs. These taxes are all designed to 'get their fair share' of Prudhoe Bay, whatever that means, and notwithstanding the fact that leases were granted spelling out exactly what their share was. We haven't reached the point of saying the atmosphere in Alaska is so bad that under no circumstances will we put any money in there. But certainly we are headed in that direction."[16]

A government relations manager with ARCO commented, "Today we have to take into account our estimates of an Alaskan project's political risks, along with geological risks. We figure the tax changes may have decreased our rate of return by 5 to 10 percentage points."[17]

ARCO, BP, and Exxon had undertaken the risk and uncertainty of developing Arctic Alaskan oil. It had become apparent that the owner state had decided to live off rather than with them. Ironically, state participation leading to full nationalization had forced "Big Oil" out of foreign holdings to costly Alaska in the first place. After investing billions of dollars over two decades, the companies could only hope that oil prices would increase further and taxes would remain stable so they could pay out their sunk and future investment. Neither of these things happened.

The investment life of Alaskan oil spans every presidential administration since Dwight D. Eisenhower's and every year of Alaskan statehood. Before the first North Slope barrel reached consumers, oil companies and their shareholders had shelled out $15 billion (nominal). Two-thirds had gone to building TAPS. The rest went for exploration, drilling, and infrastructure on the North Slope. Incredibly, the early investment was four times greater than the White House Cabinet Task Force had told the public that all the oil in Prudhoe Bay would be worth. NASA had completed the Mercury, Gemini, and Apollo space programs (1958–1972)—including every moon mission—in less time than it took to find and deliver the first North Slope barrel to consumers.[18]

The after-tax real rate of return or IRR that resulted from the actual cash flows was 7 percent, less than one-half the hurdle rate. In other words, if oil companies could have predicted the future at the start, they would not have developed Alaskan oil and would have invested elsewhere. The risk and uncertainty of exploration, oil prices, costs, taxes, and inflation proved greater than forecasted for Alaskan oil.

The inadequate rate of return begs a question. What if oil companies had invested in relatively risk-free Treasury bills instead of Alaskan oil? The following cash flow analysis compares the cumulative return of cash to the oil companies from their investment in Alaskan oil to the uncompounded interest flow plus principal for a relatively "risk-free" investment in Treasuries. The difference between the returns measures the "risk premium" for investing in Alaskan oil.

Clearly, Alaskan oil was not worth the investment risk or the risk of operation for oil companies. An investment in T-bills would have been at least as good, and virtually without risk. Nor would operators need to dismantle North Slope infrastructure in the future. Not only do facilities on the North Slope have no residual value, it will cost companies approximately 10 percent of total Capex to remove them.

Thanks to ANS development, ARCO became *the* domestic oil company, the seventh-largest American oil company, and the

CASH FLOW ANALYSIS ($ BILLIONS)

		(nominal)	(2007)
Revenue			
	Production	237	386
	TAPS	63	116
	Total	300	502
Opex			
	Production	(32)	(50)
	TAPS	(15)	(26)
	Total	(47)	(76)
Government Take			
	State	(70)	(119)
	Federal	(32)	(61)
	Total	(102)	(180)
Capex (Investment)			
	Production	(47)	(98)
	TAPS	(10)	(37)
	Total	(57)	(135)
Cash Return on Investment from ANS		93	111
Cash Return on Investment from T-bills		95	101

Note: Cash flow tables for ANS and T-bills are in the Appendix.

top marketer of petroleum products in the western U.S. However, two-thirds of the company's revenue had come from Alaska. Profit margins, including all downstream benefits from marketing crude products made mostly from Alaskan oil, averaged just 6 percent over ARCO's corporate life from 1966 through 1999.[19]

In 1999, the company that had discovered virtually all of Alaska's oil asked for a takeover by larger BP. BP divested ARCO's holdings in Alaska to satisfy federal concerns of too much control of America's largest oilfield by one company. A merged ConocoPhillips eventually replaced ARCO in Alaska while BP kept the balance of ARCO's worldwide assets.

At the discovery of Prudhoe Bay, ARCO Chairman Robert O. Anderson commented about the investment climate overseas, "We'd be better off running a bank in Venezuela."[20] At Anderson's passing in late 2007, Walter J. Hickel, proponent of the owner state, wrote that Anderson "understood building a country, unlike others who just saw a get-rich opportunity."[21] Perhaps, but paraphrasing Anderson, the original North Slope oil companies would have been better off invested in T-Bills.

Fair Share

Little is more topical in Alaska than a fair share. In 1970, Governor Keith Miller (R) proposed a commission to study the feasibility of state ownership of TAPS to accelerate construction delayed at the time in the courts. A consulting firm hired by Miller discouraged the idea as un-American and socialistic. In October 1971, William Egan (D) defeated Miller for governor and took another shot at a state-owned pipeline.

Egan believed that state control would assure low tariffs and wanted any pipeline profit to accrue to the state rather than oil companies. He recommended raising $1.7 billion through a bond offering to finance and own TAPS. Egan commented to *Time* magazine in an article entitled, "Dealing with a Northern Sheik": "I simply don't see how we can consider such a huge movement of the people's oil through Alaska without making sure that the profits that arise from the transport go the people."[22]

Egan told Alaskans on a statewide television broadcast that they would never get their fair share of oil money without owning the pipeline. Egan declared that oil companies would get 45 percent of the net profit from 15 billion barrels over thirty years. That left government take at 55 percent with the state getting only 19 percent—the rest going to Washington, D.C.[23] The state-owned pipeline idea went down to a significant defeat in the legislature. In hindsight, the bond issue needed to be six times larger in order to finance what TAPS eventually cost. Despite not owning and financing a $10 billion pipeline, state of Alaska take from 15 billion barrels would turn out to be more than double Egan's early claim.

Lower oil prices, higher costs, and heavier taxes shrank the net. Absolute returns to oil companies fell 25 percent and federal returns fell 43 percent below levels forecasted in the FEA study despite 34 percent more barrels of production. As the state share grew from increased taxes, the federal share fell proportionally. The state of Alaska received a greater absolute portion of the net than the FEA had projected even with lower oil prices. The producers received less than forecasted even with approximately the same percentage take from more oil production.

In late 2005, the 15 billionth barrel of North Slope crude left Alaska just after hurricanes had shut down most Gulf Coast production and refining capability. Inflation-adjusted world oil prices spiked to $50 per barrel, the average price needed for ANS to achieve a 10 percent IRR, for the first time in decades. Gasoline prices shot up in tandem and spot shortages occurred in the U.S. Although oil prices had been too low to support

Sharing a Shrinking Net ($2007)

Category	FEA	Actual
Production (Billion Barrels)	11.3	15.1
Market Price ($/Barrel)	50.00	39.20
Wellhead Price ($/Barrel)	32.20	25.50
Net ($ Billions)	367	291
State Share	31%	41%
Federal Share	29%	21%
Oil Company Share	40%	38%

Alaskan development for decades, there were immediate complaints about "pain at the pump" and, as always, the public wanted government to "do something."

Combined U.S. Senate committees co-chaired by Senators Ted Stevens (R-Alaska) and Pete Domenici (R-New Mexico) held hearings. Senator Domenici relayed the popular belief that oil companies were using the situation to "line their coffers with excess profits."[24] Senators lambasted oil executives, launched the 30th or so annual investigation of gasoline price gouging, and threatened another Windfall Profits Tax. The scene was reminiscent of 1974 hearings chaired by Senator Henry (Scoop) Jackson (D-Washington) after energy prices spiked and gasoline lines formed because of the Arab-Israeli War. At that time, Senator Jackson and his committee publicly blamed companies for "creating a false crisis and making unconscionable and obscene profits."[25]

During the three decades between the Senate hearings, seemingly unnoticed, governments outside the U.S. had taken control of 90 percent of the world's petroleum.[26] North Slope producer ARCO, and other large western companies such as Mobil, Texaco, Amoco, Sohio, Unocal and Gulf, had disappeared through either takeover or merger.

As of 2005, national oil companies, many in the Middle East, had taken control of approximately 80 percent of the world's reserves. Russian companies controlled 6 percent and combined government/private entities controlled 4 percent.[27] ExxonMobil, often cited by the media, politicians, and experts as the world's largest oil company, is close to dropping out of the top twenty rankings behind government entities.[28] The world's largest non-governmental oil company produces just three percent of the world's daily oil and gas needs.[29]

There has also been stealthy nationalization of the shrinking amount of petroleum resource open to private investment. After the price spike in 2005, governments without nationalized petroleum began hiring consultants to benchmark their fiscal regimes against one another. They wanted to know if they were getting as much revenue from higher prices as other governments. Alaska joined the process.

At first, the state of Alaska adjusted its gross production tax to recover more revenue from the largest oilfields, Prudhoe Bay and Kuparuk. Then, in late 2006, Alaska replaced its gross production tax with a net profits tax, the Petroleum Profits Tax (PPT). At a market price of $60 per barrel, the state predicted the PPT would double the revenue obtained with the gross production tax, dropping in lockstep with declining production.[30]

A year later, an Alaska Department of Revenue study found that the PPT, although it had brought in more revenue, had fallen 75 percent short of the state's target. Deductible costs caused mostly by escalating steel prices had doubled, thereby reducing net income and expected tax revenues.[31] Muddying the waters, an FBI investigation found that executives with VECO, an Alaska-based oilfield services company, had given money to some legislators who were going to vote against the PPT anyway.

Even though the PPT would have easily passed without the corrupted votes, leaders called a special legislative session specifically to redo the net profits tax. The state used the corruption scandal as an opportunity to capture the original revenue targets anticipated from the PPT. In November 2007, the state of Alaska adopted a new petroleum profits tax called ACES (Alaska's Clear and Equitable Share), which collected even more tax revenue than the PPT. ACES more than tripled production tax revenue from 2005 levels to an equivalent 16 percent of gross wellhead value—60 percent higher than the average 10 percent collected from 1977 through 2005.[32]

North Slope producers lobbied against the increase, claiming that ACES would affect their future investment in Alaska. Nonetheless, most Alaskans, media, and elected officials ignored the companies, claiming that ANS had been very profitable. Moreover, the owner state needed more revenue from a dwindling production rate. What better way to get it than from oil companies and their shareholders, the only deep pockets around.

Just before passage of the new tax, the Alaska Department of Revenue estimated that ACES would increase total federal plus state government take in Alaska to approximately 70 percent of net profit at a market price of $60 per barrel, 50 percent going to the state.[33] The tax also includes a progressivity provision that collects more tax with higher prices. For most of 2008, oil prices remained well above $60 per barrel. In a self-fulfilling process, every benchmarking study moves the world closer to total state control or nationalization of petroleum—with the so-called "red state" of Alaska leading the way.

A few legislators fear Alaska may have jeopardized its economic future with ACES. Other leaders claim that ACES finally allowed Alaska a fair share. In reality, as the numbers show, Alaska has always taken more than its fair share.

With declining oil production, the state of Alaska dreams of another resource boom. The top contender is a natural gas pipeline to the Lower 48. After the fifty-year experience of ANS oil development, however, North Slope producers are not excited. They say they want fiscal certainty, which is a euphemism for stable tax rates. Unfortunately for them, there is no certainty when it comes to the most critical variable for a petroleum development, the oil or natural gas price. As a result, there may be "no way out" for most of the remaining petroleum resource in Arctic Alaska anytime soon, if ever.

SEVEN

No Way Out

Before World War II, oil producers considered natural gas a nuisance and flared it to the atmosphere. After the East Texas experience of the 1930s, the Texas Railroad Commission, responsible for controlling rates for much of the country's production, started to examine methods to conserve natural gas by injecting it back into reservoirs to improve oil recovery.[1] In addition, during the 1950s, large cities began converting from coal to natural gas for home heating and cooking. Like oil before, the presumed nuisance became too valuable to discard. Industry began building interstate pipeline systems from southwest production centers to metropolitan areas east of the Mississippi River to supply the growing markets.

With no local market for natural gas during the 1960s, state of Alaska regulations allowed offshore platforms in the Cook Inlet to flare small volumes produced with oil. After the discovery of Prudhoe Bay, however, the Alaska Oil and Gas Conservation Commission, the agency responsible for preventing waste of natural resources, decided against flaring large volumes on the North

Slope.[2] As a result, operators began designing facilities that could handle what would become an ever-increasing amount of natural gas. Facilities would need to compress large volumes through injection wells back into the Prudhoe Bay reservoir until there was a market for Arctic natural gas.

By 1970, several international groups had formed to study ways to transport natural gas via a pipeline across Canada to the Midwestern Lower 48. Other groups proposed a trans-Alaska gas pipeline alongside TAPS to Valdez. A plant at Valdez would liquefy the natural gas for shipment by ocean tankers to Asian markets.

Eventually, an agreement between the U.S. and Canadian governments during the Jimmy Carter and Pierre Trudeau administrations selected a pipeline route across Canada.[3] The chosen right-of-way followed the Alcan Highway to the province of Alberta and on to Chicago, similar to that once considered for oil in the late 1960s. Startup was projected for 1983.

However, plans for a trans-Canada pipeline fell apart when costs skyrocketed and natural gas prices plummeted. It was clear that there was no chance of selling Arctic natural gas anytime soon. In 1985, the federal government and North Slope oil companies reclassified Prudhoe Bay natural gas from the reserves (commercial) to the resources (noncommercial) category.[4] As energy prices trended down in real dollars for the next two decades, there was "no way out" for Alaska's natural gas.

Natural gas forms and coexists with oil in conventional reservoirs such as Prudhoe Bay. From the start, producers decided to limit production from Prudhoe Bay to 1½ million barrels per day to maintain reservoir pressure in order to optimize oil recovery. With reinjection, the proportion of natural gas produced along with oil has risen over time. The increasing gas–oil ratio has resulted in several costly gas-handling expansion projects over the years.

Initially, natural pressure pushed reservoir fluid to the surface and kept the flow rate steady. From 1972 through 1984, producers, led by ARCO, designed, built, and installed a Central

Prudhoe Bay Production

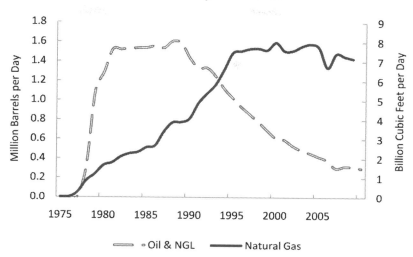

Compressor Plant in increments to handle increasing amounts of natural gas produced with oil. Reinjection of natural gas at 4,500 pounds per square inch using nearly 400 thousand horsepower of turbo-compression maintained reservoir pressure and flow rate until the early 1980s.

In 1987, ten years after Prudhoe Bay started producing, natural gas volumes approached 4 billion cubic feet per day. Producers designed and installed the Central Gas Facility, making the gas handling facilities on the North Slope the largest in the world.[5] Later expansion projects in 1990, 1995, and 1999 incrementally increased total gas-handling capability further to a total 9.5 billion cubic feet per day; equivalent to handling ten Empire State Buildings per hour in natural gas volume every day around the clock.

Prudhoe Bay natural gas contains 75 percent methane (the gas used in homes for heating and cooking), 12 percent carbon dioxide (a natural greenhouse gas), and several heavier hydrocarbon components such as propane, butane, and pentane. There are also a few molecules of mercury and nitrogen in the mix. The heavier hydrocarbon components increase the thermal content of the mixture, making it more valuable. For example, butane has approximately three times the heating value of methane per unit volume.[6]

The Central Gas Facility refrigerates incoming natural gas to minus 35 degrees F. The chilling condenses most components in the natural gas—approximately 80 percent of the propane and all the heavier hydrocarbons—into NGL (natural gas liquid).[7] NGL is different from LNG (liquified natural gas), which is super-cooled methane shipped on ocean tankers.

NGL is blended with crude oil and transported to Valdez through TAPS. As a side benefit, blending reduces viscosity of fluid in the pipeline, making it easier to pump. Through 2006, the Central Gas Facility had made approximately 500 million barrels of NGL, equivalent to another giant oilfield.[8]

In addition to making NGL for sales through TAPS, the Central Gas Facility also makes a miscible (mixable) gas mix-

North Slope Natural Gas Handling Facilities (Summer 1986)

View of the World's Largest Natural Gas Facility (1986)

ture for an EOR (enhanced oil recovery) process that combines gas injection with waterflooding in cycles. Miscible gas is mostly methane enriched with ethane, propane, and carbon dioxide in proportions based on reservoir conditions. The process applied to selected areas of the reservoir releases oil that tends to cling to rock following other recovery methods such as waterflooding.

Extensive testing and monitoring was part of a pilot project in the early 1980s. Operators injected radioisotopes in both the miscible gas and water streams to track subsurface movement toward production wells. After a year of testing, the companies decided to apply EOR to about 10 percent of the Prudhoe Bay reservoir.[9]

After NGL and miscible gas are made, residual gas goes to the Central Compressor Plant for reinjection into the reservoir. Through 2009, central facilities have handled every molecule of natural gas in the Prudhoe Bay reservoir at least once; more than 60 trillion cubic feet (TCF), including more than 7 TCF of carbon dioxide.[10] Several 60-inch valves weighing in excess of 50 tons each are used to handle the large volume of natural gas at the Central Gas Facility.

It is fortunate that oil companies never sold natural gas in the early 1980s as originally planned. Gas and water injection, NGL production, and EOR have recovered approximately 4 billion barrels of additional oil. That is nearly twice the reserves in the giant Kuparuk reservoir. Without gas injection, oil production on Alaska's North Slope would have ended years ago, stranding Arctic resources forever. Moreover, natural gas remains in place just in case there ever is a way out.

Déjà Vu All Over Again

There are 32 TCF of natural gas resource currently identified for potential sales on the North Slope. Approximately 6 thousand cubic feet (MCF) of natural gas equals the thermal energy from one barrel of oil, defined as a barrel oil equivalent (BOE). That makes the energy equivalence of all the gas identified through 2009 for sales approximately 5.3 billion barrels of oil.

An estimated 46 TCF of natural gas are in place in the Prudhoe Bay reservoir, most in an overlying gas cap and some in solution with oil.[11] The recoverable portion, 24 TCF, approximately 50 percent of the gas in place, would provide about one year's worth of U.S. consumption as of 2009.[12] In addition to Prudhoe Bay, there are 8 TCF recoverable from the Point Thomson reservoir located about sixty miles to the east.[13] Point Thomson is a high-pressure gas reservoir containing condensate, a light liquid similar to gasoline. Like liquid in Prudhoe Bay, condensate would be lost if reservoir pressure were to drop too quickly.

Some Alaskans are impatient for a natural gas project. In 2006, a citizens' ballot initiative proposed an annual tax of $1 billion on producers for "warehousing" Prudhoe Bay natural gas. The initiative lost by a two-to-one margin, but a few legislators have threatened to try again.[14] Later in 2006, state leaders ordered Point Thomson leases terminated on the basis that North Slope oil companies, mainly ExxonMobil, had failed to develop them.

The state also accused the companies of warehousing Point Thomson gas, even though there is no market for it and no way out of Alaska. In 2009, after a lot of legal maneuvering, a plan was approved that might produce a small amount of condensate from Point Thomson by the end of 2014, while injecting natural gas back into the reservoir to maintain pressure. Point Thomson would be the highest pressure gas-cycling development in the world.[15]

Throughout the 1990s, natural gas prices remained relatively flat at around $3 (nominal) per MCF. Prices were too low to support transporting natural gas from remote Alaska. In the new millennium, higher energy prices brought fresh studies to market gas as either a liquid or a vapor as follows:

1. An all-Alaska pipeline to a liquefaction plant on the coast and shipping LNG to Asia.
2. A gas treatment plant on the North Slope and a 2,000-mile pipeline connecting with an existing system in Alberta, Canada, to the Lower 48.
3. A gas-to-liquids (GTL) conversion plant on the North Slope, then transporting synthetic diesel blended with the oil in TAPS.

During months of legislative hearings in 2007 and 2008, consultants swamped lawmakers with mounds of economic studies and optimistic cash flow projections on how to sell ANS natural gas. After all the effort, millions of dollars, and months of presentations, just one thing remained certain. Every projection will be wide of the mark.

In 2008, state leaders decided to force the issue and subsidize their own project after passing the Alaska Gas Inducement

Act (AGIA). It awarded $500 million to a foreign "outsider," Trans-Canada Corporation, to obtain permits for the pipeline option across Canada.[16] However, TransCanada does not own any natural gas and needs shipping commitments from the North Slope producers, BP, ConocoPhillips, and ExxonMobil, who hold the leases containing the natural gas.

Since they were excluded by the state from AGIA, BP and ConocoPhillips sponsored their own project called Denali – The Alaska Gas Pipeline to study virtually the same option.[17] Interestingly, in 2009, ExxonMobil, the other major North Slope producer, joined the state-subsidized study with TransCanada. The two efforts will need to merge at some point. Any natural gas project would require at least five years for permit approvals and financing and another five years to execute. If all goes as hoped, highly unlikely, earliest natural gas sales would be 2020.

No one knows the market price of natural gas tomorrow or next month, much less from 2020 through 2060. Current natural gas prices, higher or lower, have no relevance to any future price. To make forecasting even more hazardous, oil and natural gas prices have decoupled since 2005.

Before 2000, utilities and industry in America used natural gas and fuel oil interchangeably for power generation. Consequently, natural gas prices generally tracked crude oil prices. Up to 2005, the price equivalence ratio of one barrel of oil to one thousand cubic feet of natural gas tended near six, the same as the energy equivalence ratio. In other words, if oil was priced at $60 per barrel, natural gas would tend to be priced at $10 per MCF.

Since then, the number of facilities switching between natural gas and fuel oil has declined. As a result, natural gas prices in the U.S. have disconnected from the oil market.[18] Additionally, natural gas has mostly lagged oil on a price equivalence basis. Since mid-2009, it has taken at least 12 thousand cubic feet of natural gas to equal one barrel of oil in price equivalence terms. Put another way, with oil at $60 per barrel, the price of natural gas has tended to be priced lower near $5 per MCF. In other words, oil is more valuable than natural gas per unit of energy.

Estimated costs for an Alaskan gas pipeline project are trending higher as well. Studies in 2001 put the project cost at $17 to $24 billion (2001).[19] A 2009 Energy Information Agency (EIA) report forecasted a project would cost $28 billion (2007). Per the EIA study, natural gas prices would need to average at least $8 per MCF to be commercial.[20] In early 2010, cost estimates ranged from $32 to $41 billion, meaning even higher natural gas prices are needed.

Ongoing studies assume marketing nearly 1½ TCF annually for thirty years or more. That means companies must explore for more natural gas to supplement volumes from Prudhoe Bay and Point Thomson. Producers have shown little interest in drilling for new oil, much less natural gas, far from infrastructure. A 7 percent exploration drilling success rate, the highest costs in the world and a tax regime approaching nationalization are disincentives.

Experience says project costs will increase even more. TAPS cost grew 60 percent from the first construction cost estimate in

Minimum Natural Gas Price versus Project Cost

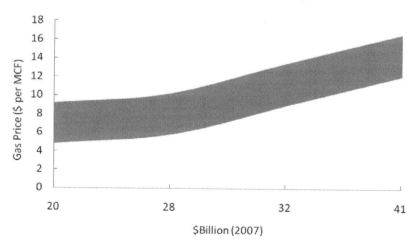

1974 through completion in 1977. Higher costs will cause higher pipeline tariffs, thereby reducing wellhead prices and net profit.

There is no way to predict the market for natural gas. In 2008, the global economic crisis dampened U.S. demand. Prices plummeted. In addition, new drilling technology has opened huge gas shale deposits in the Lower 48 much closer to consumers. Several foreign LNG projects were also coming on line. If energy prices increase enough to make Alaskan gas more attractive, other sources closer to consumers become more attractive as well.

Future natural gas prices, costs, pipeline tariffs, unstable taxes, political risks, and inflation are all unknowns. Any economic analysis is an educated guess at best. With earliest possible sales after 2020, extending thirty or forty years beyond, the risk and uncertainty are great. The White House Cabinet Task Force demonstrated just how speculative petroleum economics can be when they predicted North Slope oil was a bonanza for any wellhead oil price above $0.36 per barrel.

What is clear, however, is that natural gas is a higher-risk, lower-reward proposition than oil. A full ANS natural gas pipeline will move just one-third the energy equivalent of a full TAPS. In current price equivalence terms, a full natural gas pipeline is worth just one-sixth of a full oil pipeline.

Should it ever prove commercial, a natural gas pipeline project will not replace revenues from declining oil production on state-owned land. Unfortunately for Alaska, most of the remaining petroleum resource in the state is owned by the federal government.

Federalized Alaska

A July 2008 United States Geological Survey (USGS) study postulates that Arctic Alaska holds undiscovered, technically recoverable resources of 30 billion barrels of oil and 221 TCF of natural gas.[21] Arctic Alaska includes the central North Slope near Prudhoe Bay, NPR–A (National Petroleum Reserve–Alaska), ANWR

Federalized Arctic Alaska

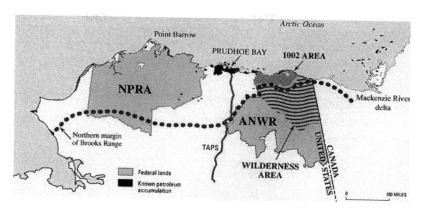

Source: USGS.

(Arctic National Wildlife Refuge), and the OCS (Outer Continental Shelf) areas of the Beaufort and Chukchi Seas. The federal government owns nearly all of Arctic Alaska, an area the size of California.

The resource appraisal does not mean there are 30 billion barrels and 221 TCF of reserves ready for production. In fact, the appraisal is based on probabilistic computer models using minimal geologic data. The only way to determine if petroleum actually exists in commercial quantities in Arctic Alaska or anywhere else is to drill exploratory wells. If petroleum is found, it must prove commercial to be classified as reserves for production.

Countries with Arctic borders—Russia, Canada, Norway, Denmark (Greenland), and the United States—are mapping the ocean floor to support national claims on potential natural resources. In August 2007, mini-subs symbolically planted a flag on the seafloor claiming the North Pole and most of the Arctic for Russia.[22] The international bravado assumes the presence of resources that may or may not exist or ever be commercial.

All commercial oil found so far in Arctic Alaska has been within approximately twenty miles or so of the Barrow Arch, a subterranean crest running parallel to the Arctic coast up to the border of ANWR in the east and under the Chukchi Sea to the west. Over millions of years, petroleum created at the foothills of the Brooks Range migrated northward through layers of porous rock. An impermeable barrier of rock deposited at the Barrow Arch blocked further migration. As a result, petroleum accumulated in various stratigraphic traps along the Arch, where oil companies eventually discovered it.[23]

Virtually all federal areas were unavailable for exploration by private companies through 1979. At that time, state and federal governments held a joint Beaufort Sea lease sale, followed by leasing of some parts of NPR–A and the Chukchi Sea.[24]

Some politicians charge that millions of acres of land leased by oil companies is sitting idle in NPR–A. Most of the leases, however, are nowhere near the coastline where companies have determined that oil is trapped. Moreover, there have been decades of fruitless federal and private exploration efforts in NPR–A. Nearly ninety years after President Warren Harding named it a petroleum reserve, there is still no commercial production. Given its history, NPR–A should stand for No Petroleum Reserves–Anywhere.

During the 1980s and 1990s, companies spent nearly $4 billion (nominal) exploring Alaskan Outer Continental Shelf (OCS) leases. There were traces of hydrocarbon but nothing commercial. In 2008, with oil prices approaching $150 per barrel, companies, mainly Shell Oil, bid $3.4 billion for federal leases in the Chukchi Sea northwest of NPR–A.[25]

Shell, the major Alaskan OCS leaseholder, canceled its exploration program after the Ninth U.S. Circuit Court of Appeals asked the Minerals Management Service (MMS) to restudy the impact of drilling on bowhead whales. The Inupiat (Eskimo) favor drilling onshore but oppose it offshore for fear it would affect their ability to hunt whales. Although the MMS had spent $300 million, the U.S. Army Corps of Engineers $100 million, and Shell another $100 million for environmental studies of Alaskan waters over the last thirty years, the Ninth Circuit called the work superficial.[26] After a well blowout in the Gulf of Mexico in 2010, Arctic Ocean drilling was again placed on hold.

The small 1002 Area of ANWR has ten times the potential hydrocarbon density of other parts of Arctic Alaska. That has made it the most attractive and most debated for exploration drilling. However, ANWR remains off-limits by law.

A Public Land Order by Secretary of the Interior Fred Seaton during the last days of the Eisenhower administration created ANWR. His assistant at the Department of the Interior was the future senator from Alaska, Ted Stevens (R). Stevens visited Alaska shortly after the decision and told a Fairbanks audience that ANWR would be good for Alaska. Alaska's Democratic leadership at the time called Seaton's unilateral action a "dirty Republican trick" and a "usurpation of the state of Alaska."[27]

In 1980, with the support of President Jimmy Carter (D), Congress designated 8 million acres of ANWR as wilderness, which prohibited oil industry activities. This doubled the size of ANWR to 19 million acres, about the size of South Carolina. At the time, the 1½ million-acre 1002 Area, named for a section of the federal act that created it, was set aside for possible oil and gas development.

In 1986, BP and Chevron drilled the only well ever inside ANWR, on Native land.[28] The well results have remained confidential, although 1,400 miles of two-dimensional seismic data shot at the time indicate geologic structures are small and complex.[29] There is no evidence of anything the size of a Prudhoe Bay and the area may be prone to gas over oil.[30] Furthermore, no one knows without drilling if there are any hydrocarbons at all.

Investing large sums of capital to search for relatively small reservoir structures 50 to 150 miles from existing infrastructure makes little economic sense on the North Slope. It is highly unlikely that the federal government will ever allow drilling in the 1002 Area of ANWR except as a kneejerk response to an energy crisis. Even with a surge in prices to near $150 per barrel in 2008, Congress never budged on the issue.

In Alaska, regardless of political affiliation, support for Arctic drilling is a given since it could mean jobs and tax revenue. Despite calls of "Drill, baby, drill" and "Drill here, drill now, pay less," historical success rates have been disappointing. For the one in fifteen wells that have resulted in a commercial discovery, low oil prices, high costs along with heavy taxes have marginalized profits for companies on state-owned land.

Direct tax revenues to the state of Alaska from production on federal leases will be muted. A study for Shell in 2009 projects that an OCS development of 12 billion BOE over fifty years beginning around 2020 would provide less than $10 billion (2007) in direct tax revenue to the state, compared to nearly $119 billion (2007) from 15.1 billion barrels on the North Slope.[31]

Although geologic prospects for petroleum in Arctic Alaska are often called the best left in the United States, there is no rush by companies to find and develop them. Rather than drilling high-risk exploration wells, producers have been optimizing recovery from existing discoveries near Prudhoe Bay instead. They are spending approximately $2 billion dollars annually to keep oil flowing and to maintain facilities already beyond their design lives of thirty years.

Even with ongoing optimizations, however, North Slope production could reach an economic minimum before 2050 without more oil. America's premier petroleum development is ending, faster than most Americans, especially Alaskans, realize. In a nutshell, Arctic Alaska holds the largest potential resource of inaccessible and noncommercial petroleum left in the United States. Decades from now, it probably still will.

Epilogue

A company will reckon as best it can, then when it finds a field will conscientiously refigure, only to find that development cost is a bit higher, prices a bit lower, taxes a bit heavier—so that it would have been better off never having gone to the North Slope in the first place.[1]
　　　　　—Morris A. Adelman, professor of economics,
　　　　　Massachusetts Institute of Technology,
　　　　　White House Cabinet Task Force, 1971

In September 1973, a research paper by the Arctic Institute of North America presented a remarkable scenario for the future of Alaskan petroleum development. The author had previously headed the United States Geological Survey in Alaska. According to the paper, by the turn of the century, two large oil pipelines would be built—TAPS and another across Canada. The two pipelines would be transporting more than 4 million barrels per day from the North Slope.

The study envisioned that, up to 2000, Arctic Alaska would have produced nearly 27 billion barrels of oil with another 35 billion barrels awaiting production. In addition, a third pipeline carrying natural gas would have been built parallel to the oil pipeline across Canada. It would have transported more than 22 TCF with another 300 TCF in the queue.[2] Following the lead of the White House Cabinet Task Force, the Arctic Institute study predicted that Alaska would become North America's version of the Middle East.

As famed baseball philosopher Yogi Berra once observed about predictions, however, "The future ain't what it used to be."[3] The reality, through 1999, was that cumulative oil production was less than one-half what the Arctic Institute report had envisioned. Cumulative natural gas exported from Alaska was zero. It turned out that Yogi was right when it came to predictions about Alaska's oil and gas future.

In 1969, President Nixon's White House Cabinet Task Force and federal economists told the public that the North Slope would be an Arctic oil bonanza. However, Professor Adelman, as quoted above, also realized that the risk and uncertainty of future oil prices, development costs, and taxes could alter their optimistic forecasts. In combination, they could and would reduce the expected rewards from the financial and technical risks associated with Alaska North Slope development. Another reason Alaska's future did not turn out to be "what it used to be" is that it is not known whether the quantity of oil projected to be in the ground is there at all. No one will know until there is future exploratory drilling outside the central North Slope.

Perception is often misleading. Revenues and profits from Alaska North Slope development are almost universally believed to be exorbitantly high. Shockingly, in comparison, the total market value from thirty-three years of production turned out to be less, by more than $100 billion (2009), than the federal government's $787 billion stimulus package of 2009. The corresponding wellhead value of America's largest petroleum development ever, before deduction of costs and taxes, was approximately $400 billion less than the federal stimulus package. As demonstrated in *The Last Alaskan Barrel,* ARCO, Exxon, and BP would have been better off investing in virtually risk-free U.S. Treasury bills than developing Alaska's North Slope.

Ironically, on March 23, 1989, the afternoon before the *Exxon Valdez* collided with Bligh Reef, in a press conference at the University of Utah, two chemists proclaimed "the end of the oil age." B. Stanley Pons and Martin Fleischmann announced they had harnessed nuclear power in a double-walled jar called a Dewar flask. Their discovery was dubbed *cold fusion.* Dan Rather led off the CBS Evening News that night extolling " … what may be a tremendous scientific advance."[4] Many believed the discovery could be the magic answer to the world's energy problems. Oil companies were taken by surprise.

Coincidentally, on that same night, the *Exxon Valdez* lost 250 thousand barrels of North Slope crude in the previously unspoiled waters of Prince William Sound. The environmental story and demands by many to end reliance on fossil fuels would dominate national headlines for months and remain in the national consciousness through years of remediation and lawsuits.

Hopes for a no-risk world powered by cold fusion plants soon faded when the discovery was debunked by other scientists. Two decades later, oil, natural gas, and coal still provide most of the world's energy. In 2030, they still will, even with a concerted push for alternative sources.

In *Media and Apocalypse* (Greenwood, 1992), Conrad Burns, associate professor at Ohio State University, wrote about the *Exxon Valdez* oil spill: "The real story in Alaska was that the cost of protecting ourselves against aesthetic and environmental catastrophes is much higher than many of us had imagined."[5] Certainly, higher than oil companies had imagined.

Exxon paid approximately $3.8 billion (nominal) or $6.5 billion (2008) for remediation and claims and another $500 million (2008) in punitive damages from spilling just *one-fifth* of the 8,549th tanker load. Total cost was approximately $7 billion—*$28 thousand* per spilled barrel (2008). At an average wellhead price of $25.50 per barrel, the cost of the spill was equivalent in value to 275 million barrels of North Slope reserves. If the involved tanker had been the *ARCO* or *BP Valdez*, the event would have likely bankrupted either of those companies.

Every twenty years or so, there has been a major environmental event involving petroleum in the United States. In April 2010, the Deepwater Horizon rig explosion in the Gulf of Mexico rekindled memories of the *Exxon Valdez*. The rig, under contract to BP, was drilling into the Macondo reservoir more than three miles below the Gulf's floor at a water depth of one mile. Macondo potentially held 50 million barrels of reserves. During final drilling operations, a well blowout occurred. When the blowout preventer did not operate as designed, oil gushed into the Gulf, causing environmental damage and threatening the coastlines of Texas, Louisiana, Mississippi, Alabama, and Florida.

Within two months, cleanup costs from the runaway well had reached $3 billion and were climbing. BP had lost one-half of its market value, approximately $100 billion, and deposited another $20 billion in an independent account to pay for Gulf restoration and compensation claims. There were rumors of potential bankruptcy, asset sales, or takeover of one of the largest nongovernmental oil companies left in the world.

Immediately after the disaster, the federal government suspended offshore drilling. Some legislators proposed more taxes on oil companies or measures that would greatly increase the cost of drilling offshore. There were calls for punitive measures against BP, including restricting the company from further work in the United States.

For BP, the real question is whether the cleanup cost incurred was and continues to be worth the potential reward from drilling. With a 65 percent ownership interest, at $75 per barrel, BP's part of the reserves was worth approximately $2.5 billion at the market. In the federal waters of the Gulf of Mexico, government take is approximately 50 percent. That leaves BP with about $1.25 billion before costs. In other words, the company had risked $123 billion (market value, remediation, and the federal escrow account) and running for a potential reward of less than $1 billion!

Alaska's political leaders used the Gulf event to call for more Arctic drilling and for opening ANWR. Some Alaskans saw the disaster as an opportunity that would bring new companies to Alaska to replace BP on the North Slope and bring a wave of new exploration. Without oil, Alaska's economy will shrink by one-half over the next few decades. Everyone, whether for or against drilling in Alaska, assumes that oil companies are eager to "Drill, baby, drill." *The Last Alaskan Barrel* presents facts to the contrary.

In June 2007, Prudhoe Bay reached thirty years of production. There were no reflections in the media or commendations from a grateful nation for the companies that had provided a reliable source of domestic energy at great risk. There was no appreciation from Alaskan leaders for the companies that had filled the state's coffers. Rather than recognizing the importance of North Slope development to the country and Alaska, in March 2009, the media flooded the public with recollections of the 35th-largest oil spill in world history on its 20th anniversary. Now, there is new environmental disaster to recognize for the next couple of decades.

A high-risk, low-reward domestic oil industry means more imports, greater trade deficits, and higher oil prices. While politicians and pundits wrestle with their views for the future of deepwater and Arctic drilling, it is time for shareholders to ask the managements of their oil companies if the rewards for the investments they are making, especially in areas of high political risk, are really worth the risks they are taking.

That last Alaskan barrel is closer than most North Americans know or want to believe.

Appendix

ANS Cash Flow Table

1	2	3	4	5	6	7	8	9	10	11	12	13	14	15	16
					Revenue		Take		Capex		Opex		ANCF	I.F.	ANCF
CY	WH	Oil	Tariff	Oil	TAPS	Gross	State	Fed	Oil	TAPS	Oil	TAPS	Nom	2007	2007
1959									0.0				0.0	0.14	0.0
1960									0.0				0.0	0.14	0.0
1961									0.0				0.0	0.14	0.0
1962									0.0				0.0	0.15	-0.1
1963									0.0				0.0	0.15	-0.2
1964									0.1				-0.1	0.15	-0.4
1965									0.0				0.0	0.15	-0.3
1966									0.0				0.0	0.16	-0.2
1967									0.0				0.0	0.16	-0.2
1968									0.1				-0.1	0.17	-0.3
1969									1.6	0.0			-1.6	0.18	-9.2
1970									0.2	0.3			-0.4	0.19	-2.3
1971									0.1	0.2			-0.3	0.20	-1.3
1972									0.0	0.1			-0.1	0.20	-0.6
1973								0.0	0.0	0.1			-0.1	0.21	-0.6
1974								0.0	0.4	1.0			-1.4	0.24	-5.8
1975								0.3	1.3	3.2			-4.5	0.26	-17.4
1976									1.2	3.1			-4.5	0.27	-16.5
1977	6.30	0.11	5.40	0.7	0.6	1.3	0.5	0.0	0.9	1.2	0.1	0.1	-1.6	0.29	-5.5
1978	5.11	0.40	5.72	2.0	2.3	4.3	0.7	0.6	0.7	0.1	0.4	0.4	1.5	0.31	4.6
1979	10.35	0.47	6.04	4.8	2.8	7.7	1.7	1.7	1.5	0.1	0.5	0.5	1.7	0.35	4.8
1980	16.83	0.56	6.04	9.4	3.4	12.7	3.1	4.2	1.8	0.3	0.6	0.6	2.1	0.40	5.4
1981	23.28	0.56	6.04	13.0	3.4	16.3	3.9	6.1	3.5	0.0	0.6	0.6	1.6	0.44	3.6
1982	19.72	0.59	6.04	11.7	3.6	15.2	3.6	2.9	4.5	0.1	0.7	0.6	2.9	0.47	6.2
1983	17.52	0.60	6.04	10.5	3.6	14.2	3.2	1.3	1.9	0.1	0.7	0.6	6.4	0.48	13.2

ANS Cash Flow Table (CONT'D.)

1	2	3	4	5	6	7	8	9	10	11	12	13	14	15	16
				__ Revenue __			Take		Capex		Opex		ANCF	I.F.	ANCF
CY	WH	Oil	Tariff	Oil	TAPS	Gross	State	Fed	Oil	TAPS	Oil	TAPS	Nom	2007	2007
1984	17.70	0.61	6.04	10.8	3.7	14.5	3.1	1.0	1.5	0.0	0.8	0.6	7.4	0.50	14.9
1985	16.80	0.65	5.67	10.9	3.7	14.6	2.9	0.7	2.1		0.9	0.7	7.3	0.52	14.1
1986	6.31	0.67	4.75	4.2	3.2	7.4	1.9	0.6	1.1		1.0	0.7	2.1	0.53	4.1
1987	10.82	0.72	3.87	7.7	2.8	10.5	2.2	0.5	1.3		1.1	0.7	4.6	0.55	8.4
1988	8.49	0.74	3.33	6.3	2.5	8.8	2.3	0.5	0.8		1.3	0.7	3.1	0.57	5.4
1989	11.91	0.69	3.30	8.2	2.3	10.5	2.6	0.5	0.9		1.5	0.7	4.3	0.60	7.2
1990	15.21	0.65	3.62	10.0	2.4	12.3	3.0	0.5	1.2		1.6	0.7	5.4	0.63	8.6
1991	11.77	0.66	3.68	7.8	2.4	10.3	2.7	0.6	1.3		1.6	0.7	3.4	0.66	5.2
1992	12.07	0.64	3.42	7.7	2.2	9.9	2.5	0.5	1.2		1.4	0.6	3.6	0.68	5.4
1993	10.97	0.59	3.20	6.5	1.9	8.4	2.1	0.2	1.2		1.4	0.6	2.9	0.70	4.1
1994	9.56	0.58	3.40	5.5	2.0	7.5	1.8	0.2	0.9		1.4	0.6	2.5	0.71	3.5
1995	11.16	0.56	3.52	6.2	2.0	8.2	2.0	0.5	0.9		1.4	0.6	2.8	0.74	3.8
1996	15.85	0.53	3.06	8.4	1.6	10.0	2.4	0.7	0.9		1.5	0.5	3.9	0.76	5.2
1997	16.75	0.50	2.72	8.3	1.3	9.6	2.3	0.8	1.1		1.5	0.5	3.4	0.78	4.4
1998	10.57	0.45	2.74	4.8	1.2	6.0	1.6	0.6	1.6		1.4	0.5	0.4	0.79	0.6
1999	15.48	0.40	2.80	6.3	1.1	7.4	1.8	0.5	1.2		1.2	0.4	2.2	0.81	2.8
2000	26.40	0.38	3.07	10.0	1.2	11.1	2.5	0.8	1.7		1.2	0.4	4.6	0.83	5.5
2001	21.27	0.37	3.39	7.9	1.3	9.2	2.1	0.9	1.8		1.2	0.4	2.9	0.85	3.4
2002	21.68	0.38	3.45	8.2	1.3	9.5	2.0	0.6	1.2		1.2	0.4	4.1	0.87	4.7
2003	26.44	0.37	3.28	9.9	1.2	11.1	2.4	0.8	1.1		1.3	0.4	5.2	0.89	5.9
2004	35.00	0.35	3.22	12.3	1.1	13.5	2.9	1.4	1.0		1.3	0.4	6.5	0.91	7.1
2005	50.14	0.33	3.43	16.6	1.1	17.8	3.7	1.8	1.3		1.3	0.3	9.4	0.94	9.9
Totals	15.66	15.11	4.17	236.6	63.0	299.6	70.0	32.0	46.9	9.9	32.3	15.1	93.4		111.0

Notes for ANS Cash Flow Table

Column 1 is calendar year.

Column 2 is wellhead price in $ per barrel (nominal) from the Alaska Department of Revenue (ADOR) Tax Division: http://www.tax.alaska.gov/programs/oil/oilprices/answell.aspx.

Column 3 is production in billion barrels from the Alaska Department of Natural Resources, Division of Oil and Gas, 2007 Annual Report, 3-20: http://www.dog.dnr.state.ak.us/oil/products/publications/annual/2007_annual_report/3_Hist-Proj_2007.pdf.

Column 4 is TAPS tariff in $ per barrel (nominal) converted from fiscal to calendar years from ADOR Tax Division, Fall 1995 Revenue Sources Book, 17, and Fall 2007 Revenue Sources Book, 108: http://www.tax.alaska.gov/programs/sourcebook/index.aspx.

Column 5 is production revenue in $ billion (nominal), Column 2 times Column 3.

Column 6 is TAPS revenue in $ billion (nominal), Column 4 times Column 3.

Column 7 is gross production and pipeline revenue in $ billion (nominal), Column 5 plus Column 6.

Column 8 is state take in $ billion (nominal) compiled from ADOR: http://www.tax.alaska.gov/sourcesbook/PetroleumRevenuHistory.pdf.

Column 9 is federal take in $ billion (nominal) calculated from state corporate income tax plus Windfall Profits Tax from ARCO annual reports.

Column 10 is North Slope capital cost in $ billion (nominal): Marcia Davis, Deputy Commissioner, ADOR to Alaska Legislature, Capital Expenditures Summary, October 24, 2007: http://www.revenue.state.ak.us/ACESDocuments/Bulletins/10-24-07%20DOR%20Bulletin%20AK%20CapEx%20Summary.pdf. Pre-1975 spending distributed according to ARCO annual reports; includes finding costs from Alaska Oil Price Policy -- Publication No. 95-14. Washington, DC: U.S. Government Printing Office, 1977, 253.

Column 11 is TAPS capital cost in $ billion (nominal) from ARCO annual reports.

Column 12 is North Slope operating cost in $ billion (nominal) from "Prudhoe Bay—Our Shared Future," BP Exploration (Alaska) Inc., External Affairs Department, 1997, 6, and "Petroleum Profits Tax (PPT) Implementation Status Report": http://www.revenue.state.ak.us/PPT%20Docs%202007/PPT%20Report%208-3-07%20Final.pdf.

Column 13 is TAPS operating cost in $ billion (nominal) from "Trans-Alaska Pipeline System Facts," October 1997, 106–107. The average cost per barrel used for cash flow is $1 per barrel (nominal).

Column 14 is annual net cash flow in $ billion (nominal).

Column 15 is the inflation factor to convert nominal dollars to 2007 dollars from U.S. Department of Labor, Bureau of Labor Statistics Inflation Calculator: http://data.bls.gov/cgi-bin/cpi-calc.pl.

Column 16 is annual net cash flow in $ billion (2007), Column 14 divided by Column 15.

RISK-FREE INVESTMENT IN T-BILLS

1	2	3	4	5	6	7	8	9	10
CY	1-year T-bill Rate	Capex	Cumulative Capex	Interest	Federal Corporate Tax Rate	After-tax Interest	Cash Return (Nom)	I.F. (2007)	Cash Return (2007)
1959	4.64%	0.0	0.0	0.0	40.0%	0.0	0.0	0.14	0.0
1960	3.42%	0.0	0.0	0.0	40.0%	0.0	0.0	0.14	0.0
1961	2.81%	0.0	0.0	0.0	40.0%	0.0	0.0	0.14	0.1
1962	3.01%	0.0	0.0	0.0	40.0%	0.0	0.0	0.15	0.2
1963	3.30%	0.0	0.1	0.0	40.0%	0.0	0.1	0.15	0.4
1964	3.75%	0.1	0.1	0.0	40.0%	0.0	0.1	0.15	0.7
1965	4.06%	0.0	0.2	0.0	40.0%	0.0	0.2	0.15	1.0
1966	5.07%	0.0	0.2	0.0	40.0%	0.0	0.2	0.16	1.3
1967	4.70%	0.0	0.2	0.0	40.0%	0.0	0.2	0.16	1.5
1968	5.46%	0.1	0.3	0.0	40.0%	0.0	0.3	0.17	1.8
1969	6.79%	1.6	1.9	0.1	40.0%	0.1	2.0	0.18	11.4
1970	6.49%	0.4	2.3	0.2	40.0%	0.1	2.5	0.19	13.6
1971	4.67%	0.3	2.6	0.1	40.0%	0.1	2.9	0.20	14.7
1972	4.76%	0.1	2.7	0.1	40.0%	0.1	3.1	0.20	15.2
1973	7.02%	0.1	2.8	0.2	40.0%	0.1	3.3	0.21	15.4
1974	7.72%	1.4	4.2	0.3	40.0%	0.2	4.9	0.24	20.6
1975	6.30%	4.5	8.7	0.5	40.0%	0.3	9.7	0.26	37.4
1976	5.52%	4.2	13.0	0.7	40.0%	0.4	14.4	0.27	52.4
1977	5.70%	2.1	15.1	0.9	40.0%	0.5	17.0	0.29	58.2
1978	7.74%	0.8	15.9	1.2	40.0%	0.7	18.6	0.31	59.0
1979	9.73%	1.6	17.4	1.7	40.0%	1.0	21.1	0.35	60.4
1980	10.85%	2.1	19.5	2.1	40.0%	1.3	24.4	0.40	61.6
1981	13.16%	3.6	23.1	3.0	40.0%	1.8	29.8	0.44	68.0
1982	11.07%	4.5	27.6	3.1	40.0%	1.8	36.2	0.47	77.9
1983	8.80%	2.0	29.6	2.6	40.0%	1.6	39.8	0.48	82.7
1984	9.94%	1.5	31.1	3.1	40.0%	1.9	43.1	0.50	86.2
1985	7.81%	2.1	33.1	2.6	40.0%	1.6	46.7	0.52	90.2
1986	6.07%	1.1	34.2	2.1	40.0%	1.2	49.0	0.53	92.6
1987	6.33%	1.3	35.5	2.2	40.0%	1.3	51.7	0.55	94.6
1988	7.13%	0.8	36.3	2.6	40.0%	1.6	54.0	0.57	94.5
1989	7.92%	0.9	37.2	2.9	40.0%	1.8	56.7	0.60	94.6
1990	7.35%	1.2	38.3	2.8	40.0%	1.7	59.5	0.63	94.6
1991	5.52%	1.3	39.6	2.2	40.0%	1.3	62.1	0.66	94.4
1992	3.71%	1.2	40.8	1.5	40.0%	0.9	64.2	0.68	95.1
1993	3.29%	1.2	42.1	1.4	40.0%	0.8	66.3	0.70	94.8

RISK-FREE INVESTMENT IN T-BILLS (CONT'D.)

1	2	3	4	5	6	7	8	9	10
CY	1-year T-bill Rate	Capex	Cumulative Capex	Interest	Federal Corporate Tax Rate	After-tax Interest	Cash Return (Nom)	I.F. (2007)	Cash Return (2007)
1994	5.02%	0.9	42.9	2.2	40.0%	1.3	68.5	0.71	95.9
1995	5.60%	0.9	43.8	2.5	40.0%	1.5	70.8	0.74	96.3
1996	5.22%	0.9	44.7	2.3	40.0%	1.4	73.1	0.76	96.5
1997	5.32%	1.1	45.9	2.4	40.0%	1.5	75.7	0.78	97.7
1998	4.80%	1.6	47.5	2.3	40.0%	1.4	78.7	0.79	100.0
1999	4.81%	1.2	48.7	2.3	40.0%	1.4	81.4	0.81	100.9
2000	5.78%	1.7	50.4	2.9	40.0%	1.7	84.8	0.83	101.8
2001	3.84%	1.8	52.2	2.0	40.0%	1.2	87.8	0.85	102.7
2002	2.00%	1.2	53.4	1.1	40.0%	0.6	89.6	0.87	103.1
2003	1.24%	1.1	54.4	0.7	40.0%	0.4	91.1	0.89	102.9
2004	1.89%	1.0	55.5	1.0	40.0%	0.6	92.8	0.91	102.0
2005	3.62%	1.3	56.8	2.1	40.0%	1.2	95.3	0.94	101.0

Notes for Risk-Free Investment in T-Bills

Column 1 is calendar year.

Column 2 is the annual discount rate for a 1-year T-bill: http://www.federalreserve.gov/releases/h15/data/Annual/H15_TB_Y1.txt.

Column 3 is the annual investment in $ billion (nominal), which is equal to total ANS Capex.

Column 4 is cumulative Capex in $ billion (nominal).

Column 5 is annual interest in $ billion (nominal) from the investment in T-bills.

Column 6 is the assumed annual federal corporate income tax rate.

Column 7 is after-tax interest in $ billion (nominal).

Column 8 is cash return in $ billion (nominal), which is cumulative Capex (investment) plus the cumulative after-tax interest (uncompounded).

Column 9 is the inflation factor to convert nominal dollars to 2007 dollars from U.S. Department of Labor, Bureau of Labor Statistics Inflation Calculator: http://data.bls.gov/cgi-bin/cpi-calc.pl.

Column 10 is cash return in $ billion (2007), which is Column 8 divided by Column 9.

Endnotes

Notes
All URLs were accessible at printing.

Chapter 1—Profits Trilemma
1. Terrence M. Cole. Report from the University of Alaska website "Blinded by Riches: The Permanent Funding Problem and the Prudhoe Bay Effect," January, 2004, p.109. http://www.alaskaneconomy.uaa.alaska.edu/Publications/blindedbyriches.pdf.
2. Scott Goldsmith. "How Oil Has Transformed the Alaskan Economy." UAA Institute of Social and Economic Research, April, 2009, p.12. http://www.iser.uaa.alaska.edu/Publications/Importanceofoil.pdf.
3. "Landmarks in Permanent Fund History," Alaska Permanent Fund Corporation website. http://www.apfc.org/home/Content/aboutFund/fundHistory.cfm.
4. Scott Goldsmith. "How Oil Has Transformed the Alaskan Economy," July 2009, p.8. http://www.iser.uaa.alaska.edu/presentations/Imp_Oil_AnchorageChamberNotes.pdf.

5. James A. Oliver. *The Bering Strait Crossing: A 21st Century Frontier between East and West* (Philadelphia: Information Architects), 2006, pp.19, 40, 82.
6. Valdez Museum & Historical Archive: Short History. http://www.valdezmuseum.org/index.cfm?section=history&page=Short-History.
7. L. H. Neatby. "Franklin, Sir John." The Canadian Encyclopedia. http://www.thecanadianencyclopedia.com/index.cfm?PgNm=TCE&Params=A1ARTA0003029.
8. John Franklin. *Sir John Franklin's Journals and Correspondence: Second Arctic Land Expedition, 1825–1827* (Toronto: Champlain Society, 1998), p.106.
9. "Sir John Franklin: Lost and Found." Princeton University library. http://libweb5.princeton.edu/visual_materials/maps/websites/northwest-passage/franklin-lostfound.htm.
10. "People," *Time*, November 14, 1977. http://www.time.com/time/magazine/article/0,9171,912020,00.html.
11. "Alaska – History and Heritage," *Smithsonian*, November 6, 2007. http://www.smithsonianmag.com/travel/destination-hunter/north-america/united-states/west/alaska/alaska-history-heritage.html.
12. Meeting of Frontiers: Gallery – Russia and the Sale of Alaska. Global Gateway: World Culture & Resources (Library of Congress). http://international.loc.gov/intldl/mtfhtml/mfak/mfaksale_grussia.html.
13. Ibid.
14. Hugo S. Cunningham. "Gold and Silver Standards." http://www.cyberussr.com/hcunn/gold-std.html.
15. James L. Swanson. *Manhunt: The 12-Day Chase for Lincoln's Killer* (New York: William Morrow, 2006), pp.49–61.
16. William H. Seward. "Citizens of Alaska, Fellow Citizens of the United States,": Alaska State Library. http://library.state.ak.us/hist/fulltext/ASL-F907.S38-1869.htm.
17. "Alaska – Report of the Government Agent – The Real Cost of the Purchase." *New York Times* archives, January 19, 1870. http://query.nytimes.com/gst/abstract.html?res=9500E7D7173BE63BBC4152DFB766838B669FDE.
18. W. H. Dall. "Is Alaska a Paying Investment?" *Harper's New Monthly*, January 1872, pp.252–257. http://www.harpers.org/archive/1872/01/0042787.

19. "Garfield on Seward: An Eloquent Tribute — The Theory of the Alaska Purchase." *New York Times* archives, June 30, 1880. http://query.nytimes.com/gst/abstract.html?res= 9B05EFD6173FEE3ABC4850DFB066838B699FDE.
20. Terrence M. Cole. "Blinded by Riches," p.17.
21. Carl Benson. "Alaska's Size in Perspective." Alaska Science Forum, Geophysical Institute of the University of Alaska, Fairbanks. http://www.gi.alaska.edu/ScienceForum/ASF14/ 1404.html.
22. Harvey M. Jacobs and Brian H. Hirsch. "Indigenous land tenure and land use in Alaska: community impacts of the Alaska Native Claims Settlement Act." MINDS@UW website. http://minds.wisconsin.edu/handle/1793/21937.
23. "The Government has big plans for developing Alaska; Secretary Lane says the building of the new railroad is the first step toward opening up that country." *New York Times* archives, March 22, 1914. http://query.nytimes.com/gst/ abstract.html?res=990CE2DB1E39E633A25751C2A9659C94 6596D6CF.
24. "Alaska's Future." *New York Times* archives, November 13, 1921. http://query.nytimes.com/gst/abstract.html?res=9B07 EFDD143AE532A25750C1A9679D946095D6CF.
25. "Land Ownership in Alaska." Division of Mining, Land & Water, Alaska Department of Natural Resources. http://dnr .alaska.gov/mlw/factsht.
26. "Class Notes, Alaska's Landlord,": Harvard Law Bulletin Fall 1997. http://www.law.harvard.edu/news/bulletin/backissues/ fall97/classnotes/.
27. The Alaska Poll: Dittman Research & Communications Corporation. "Looking at Alaska — National Opinion of Alaska Survey," Appendix B, p.1. http://www.dittmanresearch.com/ drc_researchresults.htm.
28. Robert E. King. Wrangell – St. Elias National Park & Preserve – People section (U.S. National Park Service). Alaska's "Lewis and Clark Expedition." http://www.nps.gov/wrst/ historyculture/upload/Allen%20Expedition.pdf.
29. Tappan Adney. *The Klondike Stampede* (Vancouver: UBC Press, 1994), pp.414–417.
30. Melody Webb Grauman. "Kennecott: Alaskan Origins of a Copper Empire, 1900–1938," *Western Historical Quarterly* 9, no. 2 (April 1978), pp.198, 201, 210.

31. "Alaska: An Empire in Need of People; Its vast mineral wealth only waiting to be developed, says Daniel Guggenheim." *New York Times* archives, May 30, 1910. http://query.nytimes.com/gst/abstract.html?res= 9505EED61139E333A25753C3A9639C946196D6CF.
32. Terrence M. Cole. "Blinded by Riches," pp.45–46.
33. Terrence M. Cole. "Blinded by Riches," pp.49–50.
34. Terrence M. Cole. "Blinded by Riches," p.74.
35. Terrence M. Cole. "Blinded by Riches," p.75.
36. "Smith Explains Statehood Opposition." *Anchorage Daily News*. Vintage 1958 Edition, C12, May 18, 2008.
37. Walter J. Hickel. *Crisis in the Commons: The Alaska Solution* (Washington D.C.: ICS Press, 2002), pp.4–9.
38. Lawrence E. Davies. "Alaska Economy at Critical Point; Need for Development Cited – Planners Gloomy, but Governor is Optimistic." *New York Times* archives, August 2, 1960. http://select.nytimes.com/gst/abstract.html?res= F00B15F73B5A1A7A93C0A91783D85F448685F9&scp=1&sq =Alaska%20Economy%20at%20Critical%20point&st=cse.
39. Jack Roderick. *Crude Dreams: A Personal History of Oil in Alaska* (Fairbanks: Epicenter Press, 1997), p.100.
40. "Legislative Action." *Oil&Gas Journal,* August 10, 1970, p.135.
41. "Local Politics." *Oil&Gas Journal,* August 10, 1970, p.145.

Chapter 2 – Looking for Prudhoe

1. "Tectonic Plates, Divergent, Convergent, and Transform Boundaries." California Institute of Technology, Tectonics Observatory, April 2009. http://www.tectonics.caltech.edu/ images/maps/plates.pdf.
2. Roger N. Anderson. "Why is oil usually found in deserts and Arctic areas?" *Scientific America,* January 16, 2006. http://www.scientificamerican.com/article.cfm?id=why-is -oil-usually-found.
3. UAF Seismology Department, FAQ. Alaska Earthquake Information Center. http://www.aeic.alaska.edu/html _docs/faq.html.
4. William Broad. "Long-Term Global Forecast? Fewer Continents." *New York Times,* January 9, 2007. http://www .nytimes.com/2007/01/09/science/09geo.html.
5. E.R. Brumbaugh. "Creativity, Elephant Hunt, Globalization, Doodle Buggers, and Useful Quotes – Commentaries,"

Article #70004 (2001). Search and Discovery. http://www
.searchanddiscovery.net/documents/brumbaugh/index
.htm?q=%2Btext%3Abrumbaugh.

6. "Petroleum – World Distribution of Oil," Britannica Online
Encyclopedia. http://www.britannica.com/EBchecked/
topic/454269/petroleum/50717/World-distribution-of-oil.

7. Prudhoe Bay Fact Sheet. BP Global. http://www.bp.com/
liveassets/bp_internet/us/bp_us_english/STAGING/local
_assets/downloads/a/A03_prudhoe_bay_fact_sheet.pdf.

8. Kenneth S. Deffeyes. *Beyond Oil: the View from Hubbert's
Peak* (New York: Hill and Wang, 2006), 2006, p.15.

9. Carl Johns. "The History and Status of Chemistry in Petroleum Research." *Industrial and Engineering Chemistry* 15
(1923), p.446.

10. Robert O. Anderson. *Fundamentals of the Petroleum Industry*
(Norman: University of Oklahoma Press, 1984), pp. 4–8.

11. Chevron press release: "ChevronTexaco Announces Discovery in Deepwater Gulf of Mexico," September 7, 2004.
http://www.chevron.com/news/press/Release/?id=2004
-09-07.

12. BP press release: "BP Announces Giant Oil Discovery in the
Gulf of Mexico," September 2, 2009. http://www.bp.com/
genericarticle.do?categoryId=2012968&contentId=7055818.

13. Robert O. Anderson. *Fundamentals of the Petroleum Industry*,
p.19.

14. Morris A. Adelman. "The Real Oil Problem." Paper from the
Social Science Research Network, Regulation 27 (2004), p.1.
http://papers.ssrn.com/sol3/paperscfm?abstract_id=545042.

15. United States Geological Survey Circular 1050 – "The 1920s."
http://pubs.usgs.gov/circular/c1050/1920s.htm.

16. Ruth Sheldon Knowles. *The Greatest Gamblers: The Epic of
American Oil Exploration* (Norman, Oklahoma: University of
Oklahoma Press, 1980), pp. iv, 315.

17. Agriculture Demographics, U.S. Environmental Protection
Agency website. http://www.epa.gov/oecaagct/ag101/
demographics.html.

18. "Petroleum in Alaska; Vast Deposits of Coal and Oil Discovered Near the Coast." *New York Times* archives, July 14, 1897.
http://query.nytimes.com/gst/abstract.html?res=950DE0D9
1E3DE433A25757C1A9619C94669ED7CF.

19. "Coal and Oil in Alaska; Company Organized at Seattle to
Develop the New Fields." *New York Times* archives, July 17,

1897. http://query.nytimes.com/gst/abstract.html?res=9406 E5D8143DE633A25754C1A9619C94669ED7CF&scp=1&sq= Coal%20and%20Oil%20in%20Alaska&st=cse.

20. "Alaska Oil Development; a Canadian and English Syndicate Gains Control of the Large Kayak Fields." *New York Times* archives, June 17, 1903. http://query.nytimes.com/ gst/abstract.html?res=9D06E1DF1F3BEE33A25754C1A9609 C946297D6CF.

21. Jack Roderick. *Crude Dreams: A Personal History of Oil in Alaska* (Fairbanks: Epicenter Press, 1997), pp.37–71.

22. Alan L. Olmstead and Paul Rhode. "Rationing without Government: The West Coast Gas Famine of 1920." *American Economic Review* 75, no. 5 (December 1985), pp.1044– 1055. http://www.jstor.org/stable/1818644.

23. Jack Roderick. *Crude Dreams: A Personal History of Oil in Alaska*, p.20.

24. "To Seek Oil in Alaska; Standard Oil of California Said to Have Expedition Underway." *New York Times* archives, July 13, 1921. http://query.nytimes.com/gst/abstract.html ?res=9E00E0DD173EEE3ABC4B52DFB166838A639EDE.

25. "New Era for Alaska; Governor Scott C. Bone Tells What He Thinks Is Needed For The Territory." *New York Times* archives, March 12, 1922. http://query.nytimes.com/gst/ abstract.html?res=9D04E5DC1E3EEE3ABC4A52DFB566838 9639EDE.

26. "Pays Tribute to Scenic Beauty." *New York Times* archives, July 28, 1923. http://select.nytimes.com/gst/abstract.html ?res=F10E13FB3F5416738DDDA10A94DF405B838EF1D3 &scp=1&sq=Pays%20Tribute%20to%20Scenic%20Beauty &st=cse.

27. "Boom Town Scenes Repeated in Texas; Discovery of Oil Turns Little Hamlet Into Near Metropolis and Enriches Widow." *New York Times* archives, November 3, 1929. http://select.nytimes.com/gst/abstract.html?res=F70613FB3 554127A93C1A9178AD95F4D8285F9&scp=1&sq=boom %20town%20scenes&st=cse.

28. "East Texas, Poor Many Years, Now Flowing with 'Black Gold'. *New York Times* archives, July 5, 1931. http://select .nytimes.com/gst/abstract.html?res=F60F17F6395F11738DD DAC0894DF405B818FF1D3&scp=1&sq=East%2Texas %2Poor%20many%20years&st=cse.

29. Harvey O'Connor. *The Empire of Oil* (New York: Monthly Review Press, New York, 1955), pp.45–49.
30. "East Texas Oilfield." Handbook of Texas Online. http://www.tshaonline.org/handbook/online/articles/EE/doe1.html.
31. Robert O. Anderson. *Fundamentals of the Petroleum Industry*, p.300.
32. "East Texas Oilfield." Handbook of Texas Online. http://www.tshaonline.org/handbook/online/articles/EE/doe1.html.
33. Claire Fitzpatrick and Mike Utsler. ACES Documents, Presentation to House Oil and Gas – BP, October 22, 2007, pp.6,9. http://www.revenue.state.ak.us/ACES_revenue.htm.
34. Matthew R. Simmons. *Twilight in the Desert: The Coming Saudi Oil Shock and the World Economy* (New York, NY: Wiley, 2006), p.5.
35. Robert O. Anderson. *Fundamentals of the Petroleum Industry*, pp.48–50.
36. Fred A. Seaton. "Industry Has Wrought Vast Changes." *New York Times* archives, May 31, 1959. http://select.nytimes.com/gst/abstract.html?res=F40712F83D5F1A7B93C3AA178ED85F4D8585F9&scp=3&sq=Fred+Seaton+1959&st=p.
37. Table 5.2: Crude Oil Production and Crude Oil Well Productivity, 1954–2008. Energy Information Administration (EIA). Official energy statistics from the U.S. Government website. http://www.eia.doe.gov/emeu/aer/txt/ptb0502.html.
38. The Oil Drum: Europe. "Saudi Production Laid Bare." http://europe.theoildrum.com/node/2372.
39. Robert M. Bone and Robert J. Mahnic. "Norman Wells: The Oil Center of the Northwest Territories." *Arctic* 37, no. 1 (March 1984): pp.53–54. http://pubs.aina.ucalgary.ca/arctic/Arctic37-1-53.pdf.
40. Murray Lundberg. "The Canol Project: Oil for Victory." ExploreNorth website. http://explorenorth.com/library/yafeatures/bl-canol.htm.
41. Fred Graham. "Seabees Drilling for Oil in Alaska; They Seek Petroleum Under Ice, Snow and Rock 5 Degrees North of Arctic Circle." *New York Times* archives, November 13, 1945. http://select.nytimes.com/gst/abstract.html?res=F10A14F83D5516738FDDAA0994D9415B8588F1D3&scp=1&sq=Seabees%20Drilling&st=cse.

42. Hanson W. Baldwin. "Black Gold in the Arctic; At Point Barrow, Alaska's northern tip, the Navy probes a potential oil reserve." *New York Times* archives, June 12, 1949. http://select.nytimes.com/gst/abstract.html?res=F40D1EF7385915 7A93C0A8178DD85F4D8485F9&scp=1&sq=Black+Gold+in +the+Arctic&st=p.
43. Benjamin Zycher. The Concise Encyclopedia of Economics: OPEC. Library of Economics and Liberty website. http://www.econlib.org/library/Enc/OPEC.html.
44. Charles S. Jones. *From the Rio Grande to the Arctic: The Story of the Richfield Oil Corporation* (Norman: University of Oklahoma Press, 1972), pp.294–298.
45. Jack Roderick. *Crude Dreams*, p.124.
46. Henry Longhurst. *Adventure in Oil: the Story of British Petroleum* (London: Sidgwick & Jackson, 1959).
47. Bill Stephens. "The Big Turn On." *ARCOspark*, June 24, 1977, p.6.
48. Jack Roderick. *Crude Dreams*, p.221.
49. Morris A. Adelman. *Alaskan Oil: Costs & Supply* (Connecticut: Praeger, 1971), p.32.

Chapter 3 – Great Alaska Oil Rush

1. "Amber Gris" website; description and history of whales and ambergris blocks, selling ambergris. http://www.ambre-gris .com/ambre_gris_us.htm.
2. John Bockstoce. "From Davis Strait to Bering Strait: The Arrival of the Commercial Whaling Fleet in North America's Western Arctic." *Arctic* 37 (1984): pp.528–532. http://pubs .aina.ucalgary.ca/arctic/Arctic37-4-528.pdf.
3. "Alaska History and Cultural Studies, Northwest and Arctic, 1732–1871, Age of Arctic Exploration and Whaling." http://www.akhistorycourse.org/articles/article.php?artID=64.
4. Douglas Chadwick. "Orcas Unmasked." *National Geographic*, April, 2005. http://ngm.nationalgeographic.com/2005/04/orcas/chadwick-text.
5. Daniel Yergin. *The Prize: The Epic Quest for Oil, Money, and Power* (New York, NY: Simon & Schuster, 1991), p.29.
6. Walter J. Hickel. *Crisis in the Commons: Alaska Solution* (Washington D.C.: ICS Press, 2002), p.101.
7. Lawrence E. Davies. "Oil Fever Whips across Rugged Slopes of Alaska." *New York Times* archives, September 3, 1968.

http://select.nytimes.com/gst/abstract.html?res=F70616FE3
55C147493C1A91782D85F4C8685F9&scp=1&sq=Oil
%20Fever%20Whips%20Across&st=cse.

8. Charles S. Jones. *From the Rio Grande to the Arctic: The Story of the Richfield Oil Corporation*, p.328.

9. Lawrence E. Davies. "Oil Fever Whips across Rugged Slopes of Alaska." *New York Times* archives, September 3, 1968. http://select.nytimes.com/gst/abstract.html?res=F70616FE3 55C147493C1A91782D85F4C8685F9&scp=1&sq=Oil%20 Fever%20Whips%20Across&st=cse.

10. Morris A. Adelman. *Alaskan Oil: Costs & Supply*, p.32.

11. Robert A. Wright. "Market Place: Rumors and Oil and Up, Up, Up." *New York Times* archives, July 10, 1968. http://select .nytimes.com/gst/abstract.html?res=F00E13FC3854157493C 2A8178CD85F4C8685F9&scp=1&sq=Market%20Place %20Rumors%20and%20Oil&st=cse.

12. Morris A. Adelman. *Alaskan Oil: Costs & Supply*, p.38.

13. William D. Smith. "Arab Oil Bloc Sees No Threat in Alaskan Deposit; Venezuelan Spokesman Says Export Cost Would Be High; Parra Asserts That Group Does Not Plan to Nationalize." *New York Times* archives, September 7, 1968. http:// select.nytimes.com/gst/abstract.html?res=FB0A15F83F5914 7493C5A91782D85F4C8685F9&scp=1&sq=Arab%20Oil %20Bloc%20sees%20no%20threat%20&st=cse.

14. William D. Smith. "Jersey Standard's Leader Meets the Issues Head-on; Esso Chief Sees Need For Oil Import Curb." *New York Times* archives, December 15, 1968. http://select .nytimes.com/gst/abstract.html?res=F70E11FB395F127A93C 7A81789D95F4C8685F9&scp=1&sq=Jersey%20Standard's %20Leader&st=cse.

15. Morris A. Adelman. *Alaskan Oil: Costs & Supply*, p.66.

16. "Northwest Passage." *National Geographic*, August 1990, p.15.

17. William D. Smith. "Tanker Leaves to Conquer Fabled Northwest Passage." *New York Times* archives, August 25, 1969. http://select.nytimes.com/gst/abstract.html?res=F20D16F73 8551B7B93C7AB1783D85F4D8685F9&scp=1&sq=Tanker %20leaves%20to%20conquer&st=cse.

18. William S. Ellis. "Will Oil and Tundra Mix?" *National Geographic*, October 1971, p.499.

19. "Northwest Passage." *National Geographic*, August 1990, p.23.

20. Morris A. Adelman. *Alaskan Oil: Costs & Supply*. p.68.

21. Jack Roderick. *Crude Dreams*, pp.225–226.
22. William S. Ellis. "Will Oil and Tundra Mix?" *National Geographic*, October 1971, pp.492–493.
23. Anthony Leviero. "President Appeals for Swift Addition of Alaska to Union." *New York Times* archives, May 22, 1948. http://select.nytimes.com/gst/abstract.html?res=F10B16FA3 95A157B93C0AB178ED85F4C8485F9&scp=1&sq=President %20Appeals%20for%20swift%20addition%20of%20Alaska &st=cse.
24. Daniel Yergin. *The Prize,* p.538.
25. William D. Smith. "Prudhoe Bay: Dot on Map Changing Oil World; Gravity Center is Shifting to Arctic." *New York Times* archives, July 18, 1969. http://select.nytimes.com/ gst/abstract.html?res=FB0B1FF8355E1B7493CAA8178CD85 F4D8685F9&scp=1&sq=Walter%20Levy%20arctic%20 oil&st=cse.
26. "Senators Assert Oil Facts Hidden; Three Say Size of Alaskan Reserves Is Still Secret." *New York Times* archives, July 12, 1969. http://select.nytimes.com/gst/abstract.html?res=F20C 13FC3C5D1A7B93C0A8178CD85F4D8685F9&scp=1&sq= Senators%20assert%20oil%20facts%20hidden&st=cse.
27. Morris A. Adelman. *Alaskan Oil: Costs & Supply*, p.87.
28. Ibid., p.83.
29. Ibid., pp.90–91.
30. William M. Blair. "Series of Jolts Hits Oil Industry; Not Since the Teapot Dome Scandal Have So Many Problems Faced It." *New York Times* archives, August 18, 1969. http:// select.nytimes.com/gst/abstract.html?res=F20A17FC345E1B 7493CAA81783D85F4D8685F9&scp=1&sq=Series%20of %20Jolts%20hits%20oil%20industry&st=cse.
31. Robert O. Anderson. *Fundamentals of the Petroleum Industry*, pp.x–xi.
32. Gene Kinney. "Watching Washington: Task force staff seeks to clarify views on prices." *National Geographic*, August 10, 1970, p.75.
33. Daniel Yergin. *The Prize*, p.589.
34. Lawrence E. Davies. "Alaskan Fearful on Oil Land Sale; Economist Says State May Lose Billions on Leases." *New York Times* archives, August 28, 1969. http://select.nytimes .com/gst/abstract.html?res=F50E12FE3B551B7B93CAAB178 3D85F4D8685F9&scp=1&sq=Alaskan%20Fearful&st=cse.

35. "The Richest Auction in History." Business section, *Time* archives, September 19, 1969. http://www.time.com/time/magazine/article/0,9171,901484,00.html.
36. Jack Roderick. *Crude Dreams*, pp.279–281.
37. "Permanently with Us." *Anchorage Daily News*, December 3, 2006, p.F5.
38. Ibid.
39. Robert Zelnick. "The Oil Rush of '70." *New York Times* archives, March 1, 1970. http://select.nytimes.com/gst/abstract.html?res=F70D15FC3D5B137A93C3A91788D85F448785F9&scp=1&sq=The%20Oil%20Rush%20of%2070&st=cse.
40. Morris A. Adelman. *Alaskan Oil: Costs & Supply*, p.67.
41. "Oil: Alaska vs. Mideast; Oil Men Consider Mideast Outlook." *New York Times* archives, December 3, 1969. http://select.nytimes.com/gst/abstract.html?res=F40616FD345F127A93C1A91789D95F4D8685F9&scp=1&sq=Oil+Men+Consider+Mideast&st=p.

Chapter 4 – Long Ordeal

1. "Native American Uses of Asphaltum." State of California Department of Conservation and U.S. Geological Survey website. http://geomaps.wr.usgs.gov/seeps/native_uses.html.
2. Michael D. McCrary, David E. Panzer, and Mark O. Pierson. "Oil and Gas Operations Offshore California." *Marine Ornithology* 31 (2003), p.43. http://www.marineornithology.org/PDF/31_1/31_1_6_mccrary.pdf.
3. "Blowout at Union Oil's Platform A." County of Santa Barbara: Energy Division. http://www.countyofsb.org/ENERGY/information/1969blowout.asp.
4. *Oil in the Sea III: Inputs, Fates, and Effects.* (The National Academies Press, Washington, DC, 2003) p.2. Available online at http://www.nap.edu/openbook.php?isbn=0309084385.
5. L.D Guthrie and P.R Rowley. "Containment of Naturally Occurring Subsea Hydrocarbon Emissions: A Project Review." http://www.onepetro.org/mslib/servlet/onepetropreview?id=OTC-4446-MS&soc=OTC.
6. *Oil in the Sea III: Inputs, Fates, and Effects.* (The National Academies Press, Washington, DC, 2003) pp.191–192. http://www.nap.edu/openbook.php?isbn=0309084385.

7. John Wooley and Gerhard Peters. The American Presidency Project website: Richard Nixon: Remarks following Inspection of Oil Damage at Santa Barbara Beach, March 21, 1969. http://www.presidency.ucsb.edu/ws/index.php?pid=1967.

8. "Environment: The Great Land: Boom or Doom." *Time* archives, July 27, 1970. http://www.time.com/time/magazine/article/0,9171,909525,00.html.

9. Ibid.

10. "Big Sealift Rounds Icy Point Barrow." *National Geographic*, August 10, 1970, p.82.

11. Howard M. Wilson. "Alaskan Outlook: Great – but Frustrating." *Oil&Gas Journal*, August 10, 1977, pp.105,109.

12. NANA Regional Corporation Website: ANSCA. http://www.nana.com/index.php?option=com_content&task=category&sectionid=12&id=65&Itemid=98.

13. "Alaskans Accept Land Claims Bill; Nixon Signs Settlement and Calls It 'a Milestone.'" *New York Times* archives, December 20, 1971. http://select.nytimes.com/gst/abstract.html?res=F40E13F73B5C1A7493C2AB1789D95F458785F9&scp=1&sq=alaskans%20accept%20native%20land&st=cse.

14. Mark D. Levine and Paul P. Craig. "A Decade of United States Energy Policy." *Annual Review: Energy* 10 (1985), p.557. http://arjournals.annualreviews.org/doi/abs/10.1146%2Fannurev.eg.10.110185.003013.

15. Morris A. Adelman. *Alaskan Oil: Costs & Supply*, p.23.

16. Francisco Parra. *Oil Politics: A Modern History of Petroleum* (New York: I. B. Tauris, 2009), p.122.

17. William D. Smith. "Oil: A World of Deepening Strife; Troubled World Oil Situation Worsens, as Tensions in the Middle East Grow." *New York Times* archives, June 21, 1970. http://select.nytimes.com/gst/abstract.html?res=F1071EFF3B5D16768FDDA80A94DE405B808BF1D3&scp=1&sq=Oil%20a%20world%20of%20deepening%20strife&st=cse.

18. Jack Roderick. *Crude Dreams: A Personal History of Oil in Alaska*, p.305.

19. John Woolley and Gerhard Peters. The American Presidency Project website: Richard Nixon: Special Message to the Congress on Energy Resources. http://www.presidency.ucsb.edu/ws/index.php?pid=3038.

20. Official energy statistics from the U.S. Government. Table 5.2: Crude Oil Production. Energy Information Administration (EIA). http://www.eia.doe.gov/emeu/aer/petro.html.

21. Daniel Yergin. *The Prize*, p.618.

22. Mark D. Levine and Paul P. Craig. "A Decade of United States Energy Policy." *Ann. Rev. Energy* 10 (1985), p.558. www.annualreviews.org/aronline.

23. William Robbins. "Top Oilmen Term Fuel Crisis Real; Senators Dubious." *New York Times* archives, January 22, 1974. http://select.nytimes.com/gst/abstract.html?res =FB0F10FA3B59147A93C0AB178AD85F408785F9&scp=1 &sq=top%20oilmen%20term%20fuel%20crisis&st=cse.

24. "The Senate and Big Oil Are Already Fighting." *New York Times* archives, January 27, 1974. http://select.nytimes.com/ gst/abstract.html?res=F10B10F83B5A1B778DDDAE0A94D94 05B848BF1D3&scp=1&sq=The%20senate%20and%20big %20oil%20are%20already%20fighting&st=cse.

25. Edward Cowan. "Senate Study Urges Curb on Deals with Oil Nations; Report on 2-Year Inquiry Calls for Law to Control Companies' Power Asks Deep Cut in Petroleum Imports; Senate Panel Urges Curb on Companies' Deals With Oil Nations." *New York Times* archives, January 12, 1975. http:// select.nytimes.com/gst/abstract.html?res=F00A14FB3D5515 7493C0A8178AD85F418785F9&scp=1&sq=Cowan+senate +study+urges+curb+on+deals+with+oil+nations&st=p.

26. "Survey of Publications on Exploration, Development and Delivery of Alaskan Oil to Market." Document: 100166.pdf. Vol. 13. U.S. Government Accountability Office (GAO) Archive. http://archive.gao.gov/f1102a/.

27. "Pipeline Facts, Pipeline Construction." Alyeska Pipeline website. http://www.alyeska-pipe.com/pipelinefacts/ PipelineConstruction.html.

28. "U.S. cannot afford another Alaska pipeline experience." *Oil&Gas Journal*, June 27, 1977.

29. Wallace Turner. "Alaska Pipeline Flow Set to Start Tomorrow." *New York Times* archives, June 19, 1977. http://select .nytimes.com/gst/abstract.html?res=F50712F83D5F127A93 CBA8178DD85F438785F9&scp=1&sq=alaska%2pipeline %2flow%20set%20to%20start&st=cse.

30. "The Modules Are Moving." *Prudhoe Facilities Project Group Newsletter*, December 1975, p.2.

31. "To Within One Inch." *Prudhoe Facilities Project Group Newsletter*, March 1976, p.5.

32. "United States Petroleum Operations." *Atlantic Richfield Company Annual Report 1975*, pp.11–12.

33. "Petroleum Operations." *Atlantic Richfield Company Annual Report 1976*, March 1977, p.9.
34. Bryan Hodgson. "The Pipeline: Alaska's Troubled Colossus." *National Geographic*, November 1976, p.710.

Chapter 5 – Winner's Curse

1. "The Tale of the Winner's Curse: Bidding Science Saved $$." *The Explorer*, December 2004. American Association of Petroleum Geologists. http://www.aapg.org/explorer/2004/12dec/capen.cfm.
2. "The Richest Auction in History." *Time* archives, September 19, 1969. http://www.time.com/time/magazine/article/0,9171,901484,00.html.
3. *Alaska Oil Price Policy* – Publication No. 95-14. Washington, DC: U.S. Government Printing Office, 1977, pp.7–8.
4. *Alaska Oil Price Policy* – Publication No. 95-14, pp.157–284.
5. *Alaska Oil Price Policy* – Publication No. 95-14, p.162.
6. Morris A. Adelman. *Alaskan Oil: Costs & Supply*, p.82.
7. *Alaska Oil Price Policy – Publication No. 95-14*, p.268.
8. *Alaska Oil Price Policy – Publication No. 95-14*, pp.82–88.
9. Jack Hartz, Paul Decker, Julie Houle, and Bob Swenson. "The Historical Resource and Recovery Growth in Developed Fields on the Arctic Slope of Alaska." Alaska Department of Natural Resources. http://www.dog.dnr.state.ak.us/oil/programs/resource_evaluation/res_eval_pub/r&r_growth_as_abstract.pdf.
10. Prime Rate History, *Wall Street Journal*. http://www.wsjprimerate.us/.
11. *Alaska Oil Price Policy* – Publication No. 95-14, pp.116–124.
12. Thornton Bradshaw. "My Case for National Planning." *Fortune*, February 1, 1977, pp.100–104.
13. *Alaska Oil Price Policy* – Publication No. 95-14, p.123.
14. Wallace Turner. "Federal Study Finds Profits from Alaska Oil Are Expected to Be Limited by High Transportation Costs." *New York Times* archives, December 26, 1976. http://select.nytimes.com/gst/abstract.html?res=F00D11F73F59137A93C4AB1789D95F428785F9&scp=2&sq=Alaska+oil+profits&st=p.
15. Leonardo Maugeri. *Age of Oil: Mythology, History, and Future of the World's Most Controversial Resource*. (Westport, CT: Praeger Publishers, 2006), p.122.

16. *Cumulative Environmental Effects of Oil and Gas Activities on Alaska's North Slope* (The National Academies Press, Washington, D.C., 2003), pp.24–25. Available online at http://www.nap.edu/openbook.php?record_id=10639 &page=1.

17. Bill Stephens. "The Big Turn On." *ARCOspark*, June 24, 1977, pp.3–7.

18. John M. Watts, Jr. "Where Is the Slide Rule When We Need It?" *FireTechnology* 32 (1996), pp.193–194. http://www .springerlink.com/content/x420870867408863/.

19. J.A. Middleton. Atlantic Richfield Company Internal Correspondence to Project Personnel – Pasadena, California, June 20, 1977.

20. "Explosion Closes Alaskan Pipeline; 1 Dead, 6 Hurt; Pumping Station Blast Linked to a Valve." *New York Times* archives, July 9, 1977. http://select.nytimes.com/gst/abstract.html?res =F30A11FF345D167493CBA9178CD85F438785F9&scp=1 &sq=Explosion+closes+alaskan+pipeline&st=p.

21. Wallace Turner. "Alaska Oil Flow Reaches Valdez after Delays and Pipeline Mishaps." *New York Times* archives, July 30, 1977. http://select.nytimes.com/gst/abstract.html?res=F20D13F8 345D167493C2AA178CD85F438785F9&scp=1&sq=Alaska %20Oil%20Flow%20Reaches%20Valdez&st=cse.

22. "Strategic Petroleum Reserve – Profile." U.S. Department of Energy (DOE) website. http://fossil.energy.gov/programs/ reserves/spr/.

23. "Only About Half of Public Knows U.S. Has to Import Oil, Gallup Survey Shows." *New York Times* archives, June 2, 1977. http://select.nytimes.com/gst/abstract.html?res=F20612FE3 55D167493C0A9178DD85F438785F9&scp=1&sq=only %20about%20half%20of%20public%20knows%20us%20 has%20to%20import%20oil&st=cse.

24. GAO Report to Congressional Committees: "Alaskan North Slope Oil: Limited Effects of Lifting Export Ban on Oil and Shipping Industries and Consumers," p.8. U.S. Government Accountability Office. http://www.gao.gov/archive/1999/ rc99191.pdf.

25. Ibid., p.17.

26. News Bulletin 1410: "20,000 Tankers Loaded at Alyeska's Marine Terminal." http://www.alyeska-pipe.com/Inthenews/ Newsbulletins/2009/bulletin1410.html.

27. Wesley Loy. "Tanker Safety." *Anchorage Daily News*, A13, December 4, 2005.
28. Samuel A. Van Vactor. "Time to End the Alaskan Oil Export Ban," May 18, 1995. The Cato Institute website. http://www.cato.org/pubs/pas/pa-227.html.
29. GAO Report to Congressional Committees: "Alaskan North Slope Oil: Limited Effects of Lifting Export Ban on Oil and Shipping Industries and Consumers," p.4. U.S. Government Accountability Office. http://www.gao.gov/archive/1999/rc99191.pdf.
30. FAQ about crude oil. U.S. Energy Information Administration website. http://tonto.eia.doe.gov/ask/crudeoil_faqs.asp #oil_produced_Alaska.
31. GAO Report to Congressional Committees: "Alaskan North Slope Oil: Limited Effects of Lifting Export Ban on Oil and Shipping Industries and Consumers," p.24. U.S. Government Accountability Office. http://www.gao.gov/archive/1999/rc99191.pdf.
32. New Alyeska Pipeline website: "2009 Factbook," p.65. http://www.alyeska-pipe.com/Pipelinefacts/FACT-BOOK.pdf.
33. Steven Rattner. "Owners of Pipeline Deny Inflating Fees." *New York Times* archives, June 17, 1977. http://select.nytimes.com/gst/abstract.html?res=FB061FF8395F117A93C5A8178D D85F438785F9&scp=1&sq=owners%20of%20pipeline%20 deny%20inflating%20fees&st=cse.
34. "$1.5 Billion Wasted on Alaska Pipeline, Report Says." *New York Times* archives, August 8, 1977. http://select.nytimes.com/gst/abstract.html?res=F70B13F73A5B167493CAA91783D85F 438785F9&scp=1&sq=%241.5%20billion%2wasted&st=cse.
35. "TAPS Settlement." *ARCOspark*, February 1, 1986, p.15.
36. "F.E.A. Permits Rise in Alaska Oil Price; Agency Says Inflation Adjustment Would Increase Gasoline Costs; F.E.A Permits Rise in Alaska Oil Prices." *New York Times* archives, August 13, 1977. http://select.nytimes.com/gst/abstract.htm l?res=F00715FB345F167493C1A81783D85F438785F9&scp=1 &sq=FEA%20Permits%20Rise%20in%20Alaska&st=cse.
37. "The Great Alaska Oil Freeze." *Business Week*, pp.80–81.
38. K.A. Godfrey. "Trans Alaska Pipeline. Outstanding civil engineering achievement of 1978." Civil Engineering 48 (1978), pp.59–69. http://www.osti.gov/energycitations/product.biblio.jsp?osti_id=6558211.

39. "U.S. cannot afford another Alaska pipeline experience." *Oil&Gas Journal*, June 27, 1977.

Chapter 6 – Shrinking Prize

1. *American Experience* PBS TV show – "Primary Sources: The President's Proposed Energy Policy." Televised speech delivered by Jimmy Carter, April 18, 1977. http://www.pbs.org/wgbh/amex/carter/filmmore/ps_energy.html.

2. Department of Natural Resources Division of Oil and Gas – Alaska. Annual Reports 2007, pp.3–20. http://www.dog.dnr.state.ak.us/oil/products/publications/annual/2007_annual_report/3_HistProj_2007.pdf.

3. FAQ about crude oil types. Energy Information Administration website. http://tonto.eia.doe.gov/ask/crude_types1.html.

4. Department of Energy/National Energy Technology Laboratory – Report on Alaska North Slope Oil and Gas, 2007, p.30. http://www.netl.doe.gov/technologies/oil-gas/publications/EPreports/ANSSummaryReportFinalAugust2007.pdf.

5. Mark Miller. "50 Years in Alaska," p.4. Crowley Maritime Corporation Publications. http://www.crowley.com/mediaRoom/images/publications-brochures/Crowley_Turns_50_in_Alaska.PDF.

6. GAO Report to Congressional Requesters: "Alaska's North Slope: Requirements for Restoring Lands after Oil Production Ceases." U.S. Government Accountability Office, GAO-02-357, June 2002, p.23. http://www.gao.gov/new.items/d02357.pdf.

7. New Alyeska Pipeline website: "APSC Strategic Reconfiguration." http://www.alyeska-pipe.com/sr.html.

8. New Alyeska Pipeline website: "2009 Factbook," p.15. http://www.alyeska-pipe.com/Pipelinefacts/FACT-BOOK.pdf.

9. Harvey O'Connor. *The Empire of Oil*, p.46.

10. Harvey O'Connor. *The Empire of Oil*, p.61.

11. Jack Roderick. *Crude Dreams*, pp.356–357.

12. "Sources of Alaska Oil and Gas Revenues." Alaska Oil and Gas Association (AOGA). http://www.aoga.org/wp-content/uploads/2010/06/015.pdf.

13. Jack Roderick. *Crude Dreams*, pp.393–397.

14. Leonardo Maugeri. *Age of Oil*, p.135.

15. "The Great Alaska Oil Freeze," *Business Week*, February 26, 1979, p.88.

16. Ibid., pp.74–75.

17. Ibid., p.76.
18. "History Portal." NASA – Johnson Space Center. http://www.jsc.nasa.gov/history/index.html.
19. Atlantic Richfield, 1979-1985 Annual Reports (Los Angeles: ARCO, 1980-1986).
20. "Oil: Frosting the Frozen North." *Time* archives, August 9, 1968. http://www.time.com/time/magazine/article/0,9171,902284,00.html.
21. Hickel, Walter. "Alaska's Friend Leaves Indelible Footprint." *Anchorage Daily News*, December 23, 2007. http://www.adn.com/2007/12/23/245111/alaskas-friend-leaves-indelible.html.
22. "Alaska: Dealing with a Northern Sheik." *Time* archives, November 29, 1971. http://www.time.com/time/magazine/article/0,9171,877475,00.html.
23. Jack Roderick. *Crude Dreams*, p.352.
24. "Energy Prices and Profits." United States Senate Committee on Commerce, Science and Transportation, Senate Hearing Transcript 109-307, November 9, 2005. http://frwebgate.access.gpo.gov/cgi-bin/getdoc.cgi?dbname=109_senate_hearings&docid=f:26108.pdf.
25. William Robbins. "Top Oilmen Term Fuel Crisis Real; Senators Dubious; Executives of 7 Companies Deny Contriving Problem, See Worse Days Ahead." *New York Times* archives, January 22, 1974. http://select.nytimes.com/gst/abstract.html?res=FB0F10FA3B59147A93C0AB178AD85F408785F9&scp=1&sq=top%20oilmen%20term%20fuel%20crisis&st=cse.
26. Marcel, Valerie, and John V. Mitchell. *Oil Titans* (Washington, D.C.: Brookings Institution Press, 2006), p.1.
27. Baker Energy Forum Publications – National Oil Company Study, p.1. Rice University, April 2007. http://www.rice.edu/energy/publications/PolicyReports/BI_Study_35-1.pdf.
28. "World's Largest Oil and Gas Companies." PetroStrategies, Inc. website http://www.petrostrategies.org/Links/worlds_largest_oil_and_gas_companies.htm.
29. "Energy Prices and Profits." United States Senate Committee on Commerce, Science and Transportation, Senate Hearing transcript 109-307, November 9, 2005. http://frwebgate.access.gpo.gov/cgi-bin/getdoc.cgi?dbname=109_senate_hearings&docid=f:26108.pdf.

30. Alaska Department of Revenue – Tax Division. *2006 Fall Revenue Sources Book*, p.33. http://www.tax.alaska.gov/ programs/documentviewer/viewer.aspx?839f.
31. "Petroleum Profits Tax (PPT) Implementation Status Report." Alaska Department of Revenue, August 3, 2007. http://www.revenue.state.ak.us/PPT%20Docs%202007/ PPT%20Report%208-3-07%20Final.pdf.
32. "Guiding Principles for a New Production Tax System." Alaska Department of Revenue – Tax Division. http:// www.revenue.state.ak.us/Press%20Releases/PPT%209%204 %2007%20Release%20Docs%20(2).pdf.
33. Pat Galvin. Letter to Representative Doogan from the Legislative Budget and Audit Committee website. http:// lba.legis.state.ak.us/aces/doc_log/2007-10-17_dor_letter_to _rep_doogan_questions.pdf.

Chapter 7 – No Way Out

1. Harvey O'Connor. *The Empire of Oil*, p.74.
2. "Legislative Action." *Oil&Gas Journal*, August 10, 1970, pp.139–140.
3. John Woolley and Gerhard Peters. The American Presidency Project website: Jimmy Carter: United States–Canada Agreement on a Natural Gas Pipeline – Remarks of the President and Prime Minister Trudeau Announcing the Agreement, September 8, 1977. http://www.presidency.ucsb.edu/ws/ index.php?pid=6595.
4. "Table 4.9: Crude Oil, Natural Gas, and Natural Gas Liquids Gross Additions to Proved Reserves, and Exploration and Development Expenditures, 1974–2007." Energy Information Administration (EIA) website. Official energy statistics from the U.S. Government. http://www.eia.doe.gov/emeu/ aer/txt/ptb0409.html.
5. "World's biggest gas plant operating on N. Slope." *Oil&Gas Journal*, January 26, 1987.
6. "Fuel Gases – Heating Values." Engineering Toolbox website. http://www.engineeringtoolbox.com/heating-values -fuel-gases-d_823.html.
7. Michael D. Kyrias. "Alaskan gas plant exceeds design throughput, production." *Oil&Gas Journal*, May 30, 1988.

8. Alaska Department of Natural Resources, Division of Oil and Gas – 2007 Annual Report, p.3–5. http://www.dog.dnr.state.ak.us/oil/products/publications/annual/2007_annual_report/3_HistProj_2007.pdf.
9. K.A. Rupp, W.C. Nelson, L.D. Christian, K.D. Zimmerman, B.E. Metz, and J.W. Styler. "Design and Implementation of a Miscible Water-Alternating-Gas Flood at Prudhoe Bay." Paper presented at SPE Annual Technical Conference and Convention, September 1984. http://www.onepetro.org/mslib/servlet/onepetropreview?id=00013272&soc=SPE.
10. Alaska Department of Natural Resources, Division of Oil and Gas – 2007 Annual Report, pp.3–15. http://www.dog.dnr.state.ak.us/oil/products/publications/annual/2007_annual_report/3_HistProj_2007.pdf.
11. Ibid., p.3-2.
12. Natural Gas Consumption By End Use. Energy Information Administration website. http://tonto.eia.doe.gov/dnav/ng/ng_cons_sum_dcu_nus_a.htm.
13. Alaska Department of Natural Resources, Division of Oil and Gas – 2007 Annual Report, p.3–2. http://www.dog.dnr.state.ak.us/oil/products/publications/annual/2007_annualreport/3_HistProj_2007.pdf.
14. Eric Lidji. "Democrats Revive Tax Measure on Natural Gas Reserves." *Anchorage Daily News*, October 12, 2008. http://www.adn.com/money/industries/oil/pipeline/story/553689.html.
15. Craig Haymes. Point Thomson Project Update. Presentation to Resource Development Council for Alaska, Inc., May 21, 2009. http://www.akrdc.org/membership/events/breakfast/0809/haymes2.pdf.
16. Alaska Gasline Project – Alaska Gas Inducement Act (AGIA) website. http://gasline.alaska.gov/.
17. Denali – The Alaska Gas Pipeline website. http://www.denalipipeline.com/.
18. Stephen P.A. Brown and Mine K. Yucel. Research Department Working Paper 0703: "What Drives Natural Gas Prices?" Federal Reserve Bank of Dallas, February 2007. http://www.dallasfed.org/research/papers/2007/wp0703.pdf.
19. Transcript from Stranded Gas Hearings, June 16, 2004. Alaska Legislative Budget and Audit Committee. http://lba.legis.state.ak.us/sga/0406161045.shtml.

20. "Bringing Alaska North Slope Natural Gas to Market." Energy Information Administration (EIA) website. Independent Statistics and Analysis. http://www.eia.doe.gov/oiaf/ aeo/otheranalysis/aeo_2009analysispapers/ansng.html.
21. "Circum-Arctic Resource Appraisal: Estimates of Undiscovered Oil and Gas North of the Arctic Circle." USGS Publications Warehouse. http://pubs.usgs.gov/fs/2008/3049/.
22. Richard A. Lovett. "Russia Plants Underwater Flag, Claims Arctic Seafloor." Daily Nature and Science News and Headlines, *National Geographic*, August 3, 2007. http://news .nationalgeographic.com/news/2007/08/070802-russia -pole.html.
23. Joel K. Bourne, Jr. "Fall of the Wild." *National Geographic*, May 2006. http://ngm.nationalgeographic.com/print/2006/ 05/alaska-slope/bourne-text.
24. "Alaska North Slope Oil and Gas, a Promising Future or an Area in Decline?" DOE/NETL-2007/1280, August 2007, p.11. http://www.netl.doe.gov/technologies/oil-gas/publications/ EPreports/ANSSummaryReportFinalAugust2007.pdf.
25. Alaska OCS Region – Leasing Data. Minerals Management Service (MMS). http://www.mms.gov/alaska/lease/hlease/ LeasingTables/lease_sales.pdf.
26. Tim Brander. "Shell's Arctic investment tops $3B." *Alaska Journal of Commerce*, August 21, 2009. http://www.alaska journal.com/stories/082109/bus_1_001.shtml.
27. Michael Carey. "Birth of a Cause." *The Anchorage Press*, September 15, 2008. http://www.anchoragepress.com/ articles/2004/02/05/coverstory/20040205-archive.txt.
28. "1002 Is Where the Oil's At!" Arctic National Wildlife Refuge. http://www.anwr.org/archives/1002_is_where_the _oils_at.php.
29. USGS Fact Sheet 0028–01: Online Report: "Arctic National Wildlife Refuge, 1002 Area, Petroleum Assessment, 1998, including Economic Analysis." http://pubs.usgs.gov/fs/fs -0028-01/fs-0028-01.htm.
30. USGS Circum-Arctic Resource Appraisal: Estimates of Undiscovered Oil and Gas North of the Arctic Circle. U.S. Geological Survey Slide Presentation, July 23, 2008. http:// energy.usgs.gov/flash/CARA_slideshow.swf.
31. "Economic Analysis of Future Oil and Gas Development: Beaufort Sea, Chukchi Sea, North Aleutian Basin." Northern

Economics in association with ISER prepared for Shell Exploration and Production, March 2009, p.ES12. http://www -static.shell.com/static/usa/downloads/about_shell/strategy/ major_projects/alaska/econanalysisofoffshoreogdevpt.pdf.

Epilogue

1. Morris A. Adelman. *Alaskan Oil: Costs & Supply* (Connecticut: Praeger, 1971), p.24.
2. Howard M. Wilson. "North Slope in 2000 A.D." *Oil&Gas Journal*, March 18, 1974, p.17.
3. Yogi Berra quote: "The future ain't what it used to be." The Quotations Page. http://www.quotationspage.com/quote/ 27223.html.
4. "Science: A Chronology of Nuclear Confusion." *Time* archives, May 8, 1989. http://www.time.com/time/magazine/ article/0,9171,957588,00.html.
5. Conrad Burns. *Media and Apocalypse: News Coverage of the Yellowstone Forest Fires, Exxon Valdez Oil Spill, and Loma Prieta Earthquake* (Westport, Connecticut: Greenwood Press, 1992), p.110.

Index

Between Anchorage and Valdez, 1997.

About the Author

For more than a decade, John M. Miller managed Alaskan mega-projects budgeted at billions of dollars, including the world's largest natural gas facility.

He led an international team through early design of the first natural gas project offshore China and was managing director of ARCO Norway, Inc., a foreign subsidiary.

After moving permanently to Alaska, he chaired the Trans-Alaska Pipeline Owners Committee, a board of directors that oversees the Trans-Alaska Pipeline System.

During John's 26-year career with the Atlantic Richfield Company, he handled long range planning, business development, operations, and project management in the western U.S., as well as Norway, Japan, Korea, China, and Indonesia.

He earned a Bachelor of Science in Aerospace Engineering with Honors and a Master of Science in Mechanical Engineering from the University of Texas at Austin. He has published research for NASA in the *Journal of the Acoustical Society of America*. He also served as an officer in the U.S. Army Reserve. He lives in Anchorage, Alaska with his wife. They have a grown daughter.